JUDGES/RUTH

JUDGES/RUTH

By

ARTHUR H. LEWIS

MOODY PRESS
CHICAGO

CONTENTS

PREFACE

IN THE BOOK of Judges we shall see a reflection of our own lives and times. It is a miniature history of man, the story of our human race with its ups and downs, triumphs and tragedies. But it is also the revelation of divine intervention in the affairs of mankind. Judges merits careful study not only for its lessons on the course of civilization, but also for what it teaches about the will of God. It is, furthermore, an exciting book to read; it has dramatic narratives and mighty heroes who attempted "missions impossible" for God.

Judges will show the dynamic power of the one and only "Lord of heaven and earth" during that restless period of Israel's development. At times helping, at times punishing, God's hand never left the tribes as they gradually settled into the promised land. When God's people transgressed His laws, they received the impact of His righteous anger; and when they repented of their idolatrous ways, they experienced His deliverance and forgiving love. The covenant from Sinai, basically the moral laws in the Ten Commandments, served as the standard for God's treatment not only of the Israelites, but of the other nations as well.

That Israel's faith in the one true God was preserved throughout the chaotic days of the judges is amazing. Paganism, with its powerful appeal to the sensual nature of man, was rampant on all sides. The nature gods of Canaan were supposed to provide the cycle of rain and fertility year by year, and their worship was thought to be a condition for prosperity. Yet the Israelites always had at least a remnant of believers who served the living God and conceived Him to be pure spirit, the one and only Lord over all. It was a monotheism that went far beyond the theological concepts of the ancients, ascribing to the Lord all power over the smallest details of the daily lives of men. All that came, the calamitous as well as the fortunate circumstances of life, was derived from His sovereign hand.

The judges, however, received a special power from God, a filling of the Spirit for their tasks not unlike that great power that fell on the believers in Jerusalem on the day of Pentecost. With Israel's destiny hanging in the balance, these judges performed miraculous deeds in the defense of their new homeland. The Holy Spirit's infilling for a particular mission needs to be distinguished from His work in convicting of sin and in regenerating believers.

Prayer played an important part in the lives of the people of God during the time of the judges. Only when the Israelites reached the end of their own resources and prayed to God for salvation did the answer come, usually in the form of a new leader sent by God to defeat their enemy. Guidance came to Gideon as a result of his conversational prayers; praise swelled from the lips of Deborah and Barak after the victory over the Canaanites.

Look for signs in the narratives of Judges that history repeats itself. Can you find principles that apply to all human endeavors and institutions? Is there a causal relationship between a nation's morality and its destiny? Of course one important lesson gleaned from Judges is the evil results of disorder and anarchy in government. Back then, "there was no king in Israel" (Judg. 17:6*a*), and friction between the tribes constituted a perpetual threat to their very existence.

Grave sins were committed in those days, and the biblical text never attempts to cover up the evil that men did. Gideon's ephod, Abimelech's treachery, Jephthah's rash vow, and the outrage of the men of Gibeah are only a few of the transgressions of the moral law during the rule of the judges.

The book of Ruth, however, presents an entirely different scene. Although the story comes from the same period as that of the judges, it seems to be sheltered in the Judean hills, away from the more violent aspects of the times of oppression. Ruth brings a message of love and tenderness; few people in all literature match her for these qualities as reflected in her vow of loyalty and dedication to her mother-in-law. Boaz comes into the narrative as the ideal "kinsman-redeemer" and type of Christ, a beautiful symbol of God's love for Israel. When Obed is presented to the family, we meet the grandfather of King David and discover that the story of Ruth is really the record of the great king's ancestral heritage at Bethlehem.

INTRODUCTION TO THE BOOK
OF JUDGES

THE JUDGES

THE HEROIC PERSONALITIES who succeeded Joshua in leading the tribes to victories over their enemies should not be
thought of as judges in the usual sense of the term. They
were "chieftains" in rank and "deliverers" in mission during
a most unsettled and precarious period of Israel's history.
Deborah was the only judge pictured in the actual business of
judging, or arbitrating legal disputes between the people,
and her title was that of prophetess, not judge (Judg. 4:4).
Behind the title "judges" is the Hebrew word *shophetim* (2:
16), which is rarely found as a noun but often used as a verb
for the act of leading or ruling. There were thirteen of these
chieftains who led the tribes in their battles with their neighbors and oppressors. Six judges may be considered minor
due to the scarcity of information about their lives, but seven
are major figures in the narrative of the book. Since Deborah
and Barak worked together, only six major cycles of events
are presented.

Moses foresaw the need for close cooperation between the
priests and the judges in the years ahead, when the tribes
would be in possession of the land (Deut. 17:9; 19:17).
The laws and precepts from Sinai needed interpretation, and
the common people had the right to a trial and a just verdict

for their quarrels. But the judges had more important things to do; if they did make legal decisions, it was during the periods of rest about which we have no information.

The other peoples of the Near East also had officials with the same title as the Hebrew *shophetim*. The Phoenicians used *sufets* to govern their cities, the Ugaritics had *shptn* for a similar role in government, and the Assyrians appointed high officials called *shapitum*.[1] All of these state officers belonged by birth to the upper classes of their nations and were appointed by their kings to represent them in some part of their realms. The *shophetim* of the Bible, however, were not recognized primarily for their nobility or class, but for their call and power from God. Social status played a part in some instances, such as Gideon's, but one had to demonstrate the Spirit of the Lord in his life to become a leader among the Israelites. Furthermore, the power of leadership could not be handed down from father to son. For example, Gideon's sons could not assume that they would inherit their father's authority over the tribes of Israel.

The judges were divinely appointed men (and one woman) of the people, called out for a particular crisis and endowed with the gifts of leadership and dedication. Their missions were usually local and temporary, after which they returned to their own farms and occupations. It is unlikely that any one judge succeeded in getting all the tribes and clans of Israel to cooperate in a single war of liberation, nor was this necessary, since different sections were invaded by foreign powers at different times. One judge could defend the southern tribes from one enemy while another was fighting for the people of God in the north or east.

1. John Gray, *Joshua, Judges, and Ruth* (Greenwood, S.C.: Attic, 1967), p. 202.

THE TIMES

The historical situation, so clearly described in the opening chapters of the book, fits very well into Palestine's Late
Bronze Age or Early Iron Age (1400-1100 B.C.). If one
assumes the early date for the Exodus (c. 1440 B.C.), the
period of the judges would have begun shortly after 1400
and continued to about 1100 B.C., approximately three hundred years. Just such a period was affirmed by Jephthah for
the occupation of the east bank of the Jordan by Reuben,
Gad, and the half-tribe of Manasseh (Judg. 11:26). If the
late chronology established by Albright is followed, the times
of the judges shrink to only two hundred years, from 1250 to
1050 B.C. Obviously this chronology requires more overlapping of incidents. Since, however, the total accumulation
of years given for the periods of rest and occupation in the
text comes to four hundred ten, both systems will have to
allow for some overlapping of dates and events.

There is no doubt that the Israelites were in possession of
the land well before the year 1220 B.C., when the Egyptian
King Merneptah invaded Palestine. His famous victory monument recorded the first mention of Israel outside the Scriptures:

> Israel is desolate; it has no offspring.
> Palestine has become a widow for Egypt.[2]

Israel as a personal name has also been found among the
names on the Eblaic tablets from Northern Syria, dated about
2300 B.C., long before the patriarchs. However, only the
monument left by the Egyptian Pharaoh Merneptah gives the
name of the nation during this early period. This fact, in

2. J. B. Pritchard, *Ancient Near Eastern Texts* (Princeton: Princeton U.,
    1955), p. 378.

itself, constitutes a remarkable confirmation of the historicity of the Old Testament. Of course the pharaoh grossly exaggerated his victory; the Israelites were not devastated by Merneptah's attack, as he claimed.

Archaeology continues to shed light on the times of the judges, and the biblical data agrees consistently with the historical. From both sources we know that Sidon was dominant over Tyre during the period. Hazor had been conquered and burned by Joshua, but it quickly recovered its power and independence, as is evident during the judgeship of Deborah. The great city of Megiddo, so famous during the last Bronze Age, was leveled during the latter part of the twelfth century B.C., which explains why nearby Taanach was mentioned to pinpoint the location of Sisera's army (Judg. 5:19). Sea peoples from the Aegean area had raided all along the coast of Syria and Palestine, causing one powerful city-nation after another to fall. More important, archaeology shows that the superpowers (Babylonia, Assyria, the Hittites, and Egypt) were relatively weak during the days of the judges and the monarchy. Internal affairs kept them busy at home. This, humanly speaking, made possible the survival of the nation of Israel. The smaller, local enemies were trouble enough for her armies.

Bible students recognize the transitional nature of this period of the judges. It served as a bridge, linking the times of Moses and Joshua to the "Golden Age" of David and Solomon. But it was a time of trouble and unrest for the chosen people. "In those days there was no king in Israel; everyone did what was right in his own eyes" (21:25). This did not mean, however, that total chaos prevailed. Locally, each tribe had to "dig in" and establish its own roots, towns, and security. After years of wandering as nomads through the desert, the time had come to learn farming, both as a means of holding the land and as a livelihood. Probably the Israelites copied many farming practices from their Canaanite neighbors, although this in itself was a problem since the nature gods of the Canaanites were strongly linked to the crops and produce, weather and land. Such contact all too often led the Israelites into pagan worship and idolatry.

One remarkable discovery that provides background data for the judges is the Amarna Tablets. Many letters were found in the city of the famous Akhenaten, dating from the fourteenth century B.C. and written by the kings of the major city-states of Canaan. All of them were vassels under the protective wing of Egypt. Their correspondence with Akhenaten reveals important details about the political structure and institutions of that day. One particular problem repeatedly mentioned relates to the 'Apiru. From the general area of Shechem, bands of these lawless 'Apiru would march out to raid and plunder the highways and cities. So the kings were demanding that pharaoh's army keep the roads safe for travel and punish the 'Apiru. Many scholars have concluded that the name *Hebrew* is linguistically the same as 'Apiru and that some identity between the two peoples can be assumed. However, serious social and cultural differences also existed between them. The 'Apiru were a mixed group of people—social misfits and bandits for the most part—who were not organized by tribes and clans under one head as the Israelites were when Joshua led them into the land.

Ugarit, the great seaport to the north of the Phoenicians, was still in existence when the judges began their work. From the many clay tablets found at this site of Ugarit, modern Ras

Shamra, we may now confidently describe the religion of the Canaanites and understand why it was so abhorred by the people of God. The violence and corruption of the fertility rites to Baal and Astarte; the human sacrifice, slavery, and perversion; the practice of religious prostitution in the "high places"; all have been exposed in the archaeological finds at Ugarit. When a society or nation sinks to this level of evil, it inevitably destroys itself, or God allows some outside force to bring disaster upon it. Moses said, "It is not for your righteousness or for the uprightness of your heart that you are going to possess their land, but it is because of the wickedness of these nations that the LORD your God is driving them out before you" (Deut. 9:5a). In the light of these facts we can better understand why Gideon was ordered to eliminate the Baal shrine in the center of his hometown.

THE WRITER

No identification can be found for the man who wrote the book of Judges, although Jewish tradition affirmed him to be the great prophet Samuel.[3] Certainly Samuel is a strong possibility for the task, since there are a number of hints linking the time of writing with the early part of the monarchy, when Samuel lived. That the book came from the inspired writing of some Hebrew prophet may be inferred from its position among the early prophets in the Hebrew Bible.

The writer had information about the days of the judges, information that most certainly would have become lost to authors of later centuries. He knew the city of Gezer to be a Canaanite stronghold (Judg. 1:29), but in Solomon's reign

---

3. A. S. Geden, "Book of Judges," in *The International Standard Bible Encyclopaedia*, ed. James Orr, 5 vols. (1915; reprint ed., Grand Rapids: Eerdmans, 1939), 3:1774.

it was incorporated into Israel as a wedding gift to the king by the pharaoh of Egypt (1 Kings 9:16). He knew Jerusalem was a Jebusite city before it fell to King David's men about 1000 B.C. "So the Jebusites have lived with the sons of Benjamin in Jerusalem *to this day*" (Judg. 1:21*b*, itals. added). He also knew that the "house of God" had moved from Shiloh, an event that took place during Eli's priesthood in the early part of the eleventh century (18:31).

One consideration argues against Samuel as the author of Judges: he was never enthusiastic about a king in Israel, nor likely to suggest that a royal leader would solve all the problems of the tribes. Yet, the writer of this book seems to think that a king is the best answer for the nation's disunity and weakness. So many calamities happened back in those chaotic days when "there was no king in Israel" (19:1; 21:25).

The narration of Israel's history moves without a break from the closing events of Judges to the opening ones in 1 Samuel; thus the writing of Judges must have been part of a larger plan of record keeping. A school of prophets founded by Samuel may prove to be the solution to the question of the authorship of these early historical works.

THE THEME

Some critics believe the theme of Judges can be built on the repeated refrain, "there was no king in Israel." The writer, in an effort to magnify the importance of the monarchy, used every instance of trouble and disaster he could recall from that former period to prove how much a king was needed. We may concede that this concern for showing a contrast between the days before and after the great kings was present in the author's mind. But, as a true prophet, inspired by God and guided by the Holy Spirit, his first and highest goal would have been to reveal the sovereignty of God over all of Israel's doing.

The moral laws of the covenant from Sinai play a fundamental role in the narratives of the judges. Already the tribes knew that they were uniquely a "chosen people." Their prayers and pleas for deliverance were based on this premise. From the standpoint of the prophets, this book shows its main theme to be God's providential care and discipline of His people in troubled times.

A variant of this theme would be the revelation of the purpose of human history as God sees it. A "theology of history" emerges upon careful study of the pattern set down in each cycle of the judges. Not once but over and over again, the Israelites experienced: (a) rest, (b) idolatry, (c) oppression, and (d) deliverance—in that order. Each time a different nation came in to punish Israel, and each time God raised up a new champion to bring victory. The following chart illustrates this pattern during one cycle of events:

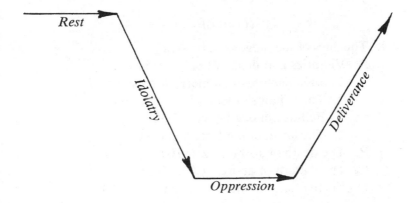

The rest phase usually lasted only as long as the current judge was living or was influential over the people. When he passed from the scene, the Israelites returned to pagan worship and practices that dragged them down to the level of their Canaanite neighbors. This degree of apostasy always led to divine reprobation in the form of war and oppression by some nation more powerful than the tribes. Then the Israelites' cries for deliverance brought God's response in the person of a judge to champion the cause of liberty and justice. Spirit-filled judges were the means of rescuing the Israelites and of bringing rest and peace back to the tribes.

This simple routine of events cannot be projected at will over all cultures and circumstances, yet it does provide some guidelines for the interpretation of history. No corrupt nation can presume upon the grace of God indefinitely; sooner or later its lawlessness will bring disaster, either from within or without. "Blessed is the nation whose God is the LORD" (Psalm 33:12*a*) is the refrain of the inspired psalmists and prophets of the Old Testament, and the book of Judges amply illustrates this truth.

OUTLINE OF JUDGES

  I. The days of the judges (1:1—3:6)
    A. Victories and defeats (1:1—2:5)
      1. Judah and Simeon merge forces (1:1-21)
      2. The exploits of Ephraim and Manasseh (1:22-29)
      3. Failures in obedience (1:30-36)
      4. The angel of the Lord (2:1-5)
    B. The death of Joshua (2:6-10)
    C. The pattern of apostasy (2:11-23)
    D. Enemy nations still in the land (3:1-6)

II. The heroic deeds of the judges (3:7—16:31)
   A. Othniel and the Arameans (3:7-11)
   B. Ehud and the Moabites (3:12-30)
      1. Ehud's plot (3:15-25)
      2. Ehud's victory (3:26-30)
   C. Shamgar, the judge (3:31)
   D. Deborah and Barak and the Canaanites (4:1—5:31)
      1. Deborah, the prophetess (4:1-5)
      2. Barak, commander for God (4:6-16)
      3. Sisera, Canaanite general (4:17-24)
      4. Victory song of praise to God (5:1-31)
   E. Gideon and the Midianites (6:1—8:28)
      1. Gideon's call (6:13-24)
      2. Victory at home (6:25-40)
      3. Preparation for battle (7:1-15)
      4. Gideon's great victory (7:16-22)
      5. The retreat of the enemy (7:23—8:21)
      6. Keeping the peace (8:22-35)
   F. Abimelech's treachery (9:1-57)
      1. Abimelech's evil plot (9:1-6)
      2. Jotham's fable (9:7-21)
      3. Abimelech's troubled reign (9:22-49)
      4. Abimelech's death (9:50-57)
   G. Two minor judges (10:1-5)
   H. Jephthah and the Ammonites (10:6—12:7)
      1. Jephthah's call and military strategy (11:1-29, 32-33)
      2. Jephtah's terrible vow (11:30-31, 34-40)
      3. War with Ephraim (12:1-7)
   I. Three minor judges (12:8-15)

1

TROUBLED TIMES

I. THE DAYS OF THE JUDGES (1:1—3:6)

A. VICTORIES AND DEFEATS (1:1—2:5)

THE STORY of the Judges begins where the book of Joshua ends, with the death of Joshua, the great leader and man of God. A full record of Joshua's death and burial is repeated in 2:6-9, suggesting that the information in chapter 1 is really a summary of the state of affairs just before his death.

1. *Judah and Simeon merge forces (1:1-21)*

The tribes of Judah and Simeon merged their forces to carry out a series of attacks on the Canaanites in the hill country south of Jerusalem and as far as the Negev. They captured the town of Bezek and punished the king, Adoni-bezek (in Hebrew, "Lord of Bezek"), by cutting off his thumbs and big toes. This was a common way of eliminating a warrior from further military service; also, a mutilated king would probably never return to his throne. The town of Bezek is usually placed in Ephraim, about seventeen miles north of Shechem. However, a Judean location would fit the situation better. Furthermore, the name Adoni-bezek may be an alternate for Adoni-zedek, the king of Jerusalem men-

tioned in Joshua 10:1. This would also explain why he was
brought to Jerusalem and died there.

The city of the Jebusites was taken by the men of Judah
and Simeon but evidently not held for long. Nor were the
inhabitants driven out by the Benjamites, for they continued
to live as their neighbors (Judg. 1:21). The Jebusites were a
mixed people who descended from early colonies of Hittites
and Amorites in Canaan. The city dates back to the third
millennium and may be the *Salem* ruled by Melchizedek in
Genesis 14:18. On the other hand, the latest discoveries at
Ebla in Syria list a *Jerusalem* as early as 2300 B.C.! *Salem*
may turn out to be another city, perhaps in the Transjor-
danian area. Jerusalem in its Hebrew form means "foundation of peace."[1] It was occupied by the Jebusites until the
daring conquest by David and his men about 1000 B.C., when
he made it the capital of the twelve tribes.

The Kenites were related to the Midianites, and many of
them joined the tribe of Judah during the wilderness wanderings because of the family tie with Moses' father-in-law,
Jethro. Caleb, the most famous of the Kenites, was rewarded
for his service to Israel by the gift of two important cities:
Hebron and Debir (1:10-20). The former was clearly
marked as the shrine of the ancient fathers of the Hebrews,
but the location of Debir was a matter of controversy until
the excavation of Tell Beit Mirsim, eleven miles southwest of
Hebron. Additional evidence came with the identification of
the upper and lower springs just to the west of the Tell; these
two cold freshwater springs still serve the local farmers and

---

1. Suggestions for the etymology of the name *Jerusalem* differ widely. Some
scholars tie it to an ancient Canaanite deity named Salem; others prefer
"City of Peace," or "Foundation of Peace." Cf. discussion by Charles
Pfeiffer, *Baker's Bible Atlas* (Grand Rapids: Baker, 1961), p. 149.

Bedouins. The word in the text is *gulloth,* meaning a "bubbling fountain," a spring of "living" water so highly praised by the peoples of the land.

2. *The exploits of Ephraim and Manasseh (1:22-29)*

Next, the account turns to the central area and the exploits of the twin tribes of Ephraim and Manasseh. From many conquests, only one is singled out, the capture of Bethel, perhaps because of its memorable connection with the flight of Jacob and with his dream (Gen. 28:19). The local name of Bethel, "House of God," was *Luz,* which may have been derived from the term for "almond trees."

Manasseh's assigned area certainly contained some of the most imposing and powerful of the Canaanite city-states: Beth-shean, Taanach, Megiddo, Dor, and others. The task of occupation was just too great, but Manasseh did manage to conscript some of the Canaanites to serve as forced laborers (Josh. 16:10). Administrative texts from Ras Shamra reveal similar use of forced labor gangs from subject peoples.

Ephraim had the same problem with the heavily fortified city of Gezer on the edge of the plain overlooking Joppa. Gezer was never captured, not even by David. It was eventually taken by Egypt and presented as a wedding gift to Solomon when he married an Egyptian princess (1 Kings 9:16).

3. *Failures in obedience (1:30-36)*

Asher's possessions along the coast should have included the cities of Acco, Sidon, and the others mentioned in verse 31, but they were never conquered. Zebulun failed to take two important cities of Galilee. The tribe of Naphtali never eliminated from its territory the pagan inhabitants of northern Beth-shemesh or Beth-anath. So reads the list of the tribes' repeated failures to confiscate all the land and to fully obey the command of the Lord through Moses and Joshua.

The tribe of Dan was especially afflicted by its immediate neighbors, the Amorites and Philistines, on the plains west of Aijalon. (Read Josh. 19:40-48 for the full account of their defeat and expulsion from the land originally assigned to them.) For a time the Danites tried to live along the foothills, but finally they resolved to migrate to the northland, above the Hulah Valley, where they captured the city of Laish and re-named it Dan (Judg. 18:27-29).

4. *The angel of the Lord (2:1-5)*

Gilgal by the Jordan had been headquarters for many of the tribes from the beginning of the conquest of Canaan. There for a few years the sanctuary rested and the sacrifices by the Aaronic priests continued. We read that "the angel of the LORD came up from Gilgal" to a place meaning "the weepers," *Bochim* in Hebrew (2:1). A priest or prophet may be indicated by the phrase "angel of the LORD," since *angel* may also be translated as "messenger." The importance of this event and message, however, suggests a heavenly being such as that one called the "captain of the LORD's host" and before whom Joshua bowed down and worshiped (Josh. 5:13-15), or, the angel of the Lord who wrestled with Jacob at the brook Jabbok (Gen. 32:24-30). This messenger, or angel, from God severely rebuked the Israelites for their disobedience in failing to drive out all their enemies. Perhaps of equal or greater importance, the tribes had failed to "tear down their altars" (Judg. 2:2). In other words, the Israelites already had accommodated their faith to the pagan

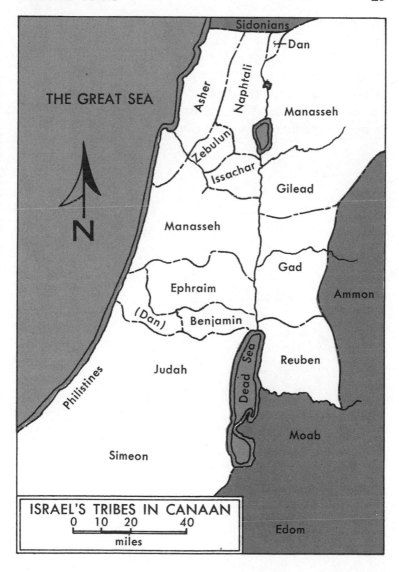

THE GREAT SEA

N

Sidonians

Dan

Asher

Naphtali

Manasseh

Zebulun

Issachar

Gilead

Manasseh

Gad

Ephraim

Ammon

(Dan)

Benjamin

Dead Sea

Judah

Reuben

Philistines

Simeon

Moab

ISRAEL'S TRIBES IN CANAAN

0   10   20   40

miles

Edom

religion of the Canaanites and were guilty of trespassing the very first commandment (Exod. 20:3). Tears of regret followed the stern words of the angel, but the people's apostasy had already begun to set in, and the damage seemed irreparable. True repentance must go beyond tears of sorrow and achieve a right-about-face, a turning of one's entire life from sin to a walk that pleases the Lord.

2

PENALTIES OF DISOBEDIENCE

B. THE DEATH OF JOSHUA (2:6-10)

THIS ACCOUNT in Judges closely parallels Joshua 24, which records the final words, death, and burial of that great, heroic leader of Israel. Joshua delivered his last plea for faithfulness to the covenant, ending with the affirmation, "As for me and my house, we will serve the LORD" ((24:15*b*). Finally, he sent each tribe back to its assigned area to complete the work of occupation and to clear out the local inhabitants and their pagan altars.

Joshua's tomb was at Timnath-heres, which could be the ancient name for the present town of Tibneh, only six miles from Shiloh. Compare the place name *Timnath-heres* here with *Timnath-sereh* in Joshua 19:50, which was given to Joshua for his personal inheritance. The two names would be identical with a simple exchange of two letters.

"Gathered to their fathers" (Judg. 2:10) is a well-known phrase in the Old Testament for life after death; it fitly described the passing of the living into the next world, where they joined the others of the family that had died before them. Simple as this concept may appear, it nevertheless speaks forcefully against any doctrine of the annihilation of the soul.

C. THE PATTERN OF APOSTASY (2:11-23)

Wickedness and idol worship are linked together in the history of the human race. The relationship of the people in every generation to their Creator has affected their conduct and their relationships to their fellowmen. When any people who knew God forsook Him, the result was a vacuum of religion that was usually filled with base objects of worship. Canaanite deities and idols appealed to the sensual passions of man, attracting the people of God with an almost irresistable force. Thus, apostasy set in almost as soon as a new generation grew up that "did not know the LORD, nor yet the work which He had done for Israel" (2:10*b*).

Judges 2:11-23 establishes a pattern of events that will be repeated throughout the narratives of the main judges.[1] Moral failure or transgression of the covenant always brought on years of affliction and oppression. Finally, when the Israelites would cry out to the Lord for help, He would send a heroic leader to rescue His people. The victory that followed always led to a time of peace and faithfulness to the Lord. This typical cycle of events conveniently prepares the reader for the specific narratives of the great judges in the book.

The Baals and the Ashtaroth (2:13 gives the plural for these deities) were especially favored by the Phoenicians, Ashtarte being the patron goddess of the Sidonians. Baal was not the name but the title of the rain-god, Hadad, held responsible for the fertilization of the earth every spring. Ashtarte carried over the years a variety of titles from moon-goddess ("queen of heaven" in Jer. 7:18) to goddess of sex

1. For a diagram of this cycle see *Preface*, p. 17.

and fertility. Her name must not be confused with the Asheroth, or "pillars," sometimes translated as "groves," where the perverted worship of Ashtarte was carried on. Archaeologists have found such objects in high places and shrines, where the rites usually included orgies of drunkenness, fornication, sadistic practices, and human sacrifices.[2]

D. ENEMY NATIONS STILL IN THE LAND (3:1-6)

Having accused the tribes of sinful negligence for not driving out the pagan peoples of Canaan, the prophetic writer now saw a divine purpose in the situation and revealed that these nations would provide a learning experience, a "test" of courage and faithfulness for the new generation that knew nothing of war.

The Philistines, from whose name the name Palestine was derived, were a migrant nation from the Aegean and the delta area of Egypt; most of them came during the early part of the twelfth century B.C. Their five capital cities are listed in Joshua 13:3, and the kings of these cities formed a ruling council over the entire nation. Philistine culture brought in many Greek customs from the Aegean area.

The Canaanites got their name from the seashell, indigenous to the coast of Canaan, from which was extracted a purple dye. As a subgrouping of Canaanites, the Sidonians and Phoenicians distinguished themselves with their merchant marine and extensive trading by sea. Peaceful relationships with the Phoenicians prevailed through most of the history of Israel. Sidon was the first son of Canaan (Gen. 10:15).

2. William F. Albright, *Yahweh and the Gods of Canaan* (Garden City, N.Y.: Doubleday, 1969), pp. 189-92, 205.

Hivites lived up in the mountains of Lebanon and appear to have been a non-Semitic people, possibly related to the Hurrians of northern Mesopotamia. Joshua 11:3 also locates them on the slopes of Mount Hermon.

In summary, the Israelites lived with all these Gentile nations, intermarried with them, and inevitably worshiped their pagan deities.

3

THREE BRAVE MEN

II. THE HEROIC DEEDS OF THE JUDGES (3:7—16:31)

COUNTING DEBORAH, the prophetess, thirteen judges are introduced in the narratives of the book. However, six of them receive so little detail that their lives and work remain obscure. These six are Shamgar, Tola, Jair, Ibzan, Elon, and Abdon. Abimelech, Gideon's treacherous son who seized control of Shechem, should not be added to this list since he is not treated as one of the God-sent judges of Israel.

This leaves seven major heroes who were entrusted with the leadership and deliverance of the Israelites. Since Deborah is allied with Barak in the same crisis, we have in fact six major stories and six brief ones to tell in this section, which runs through chapter 16.

A. OTHNIEL AND THE ARAMEANS (3:7-11)

The first crisis of slavery and oppression was brought on the Israelites by the corruption of their true faith through idol worship. "Then the anger of the LORD was kindled against Israel" (3:8a). Literally, "His nose became hot," a most expressive metaphor for anger and one of the most obvious examples of the anthropomorphisms for God in the Old Testament. Anger expressed righteousness in a situation

31

such as this: when the people of God backslide and do wicked and idolatrous deeds, they can expect such a reaction from a holy God.

Cushan-rishathaim was a king from the region of Upper Mesopotamia. His name may actually have been a term of hatred for the "Cushite of the Double Outrage." Some have seen Edom instead of *Aram* in the word translated "Mesopotamia."[1] Edom fits the context better, allowing for an enemy closer to Judah and the Negev where Othniel lived with the other Kenites (Judg. 1:13). However, intrusions by kings and armies from Mesopotamia and Aram were frequent, even back as early as the seizure of Lot from Sodom, in Genesis 14. Such a king, bent on plunder, may have marched his troops down the King's Highway through Transjordan, then moved up from the south to enslave and oppress Judah for eight years.

The reader should understand that it is *because* the Spirit of the Lord came upon Othniel that he was enabled to win the battle and subsequently to rule Israel during forty years of peace. God's Holy Spirit came upon such great personalities and leaders much in the same way that He filled and empowered the apostles of the early church in the book of Acts. In most cases, we may also assume the personal salvation of these men, but the Spirit's work in convicting and forgiving sinners is not necessarily prerequisite in the Old Testament to His work of guiding or empowering His instruments in history. At times we will come across a man, such as Jephthah, whose life shows almost no evidence of spirituality, yet he, too, was moved by the Spirit to rescue the people of God.

1. Robert G. Boling, *Judges,* The Anchor Bible (Garden City, N.Y.: Doubleday, 1975), p. 80.

B. Ehud and the moabites (3:12-30)

What Othniel achieved for Judah, Ehud did for Benjamin and the central tribes. Enemy nations from the desert rallied behind Eglon, king of Moab, to overwhelm the Israelites. Ammon was located to the east of the Jordan and generally north of Moab; the Amorites had been soundly defeated by Joshua and their lands occupied by Reuben and Gad. The Amalekites had followed the tribes all across the wilderness with harrassing and warlike thrusts, going back to the battle at Rephidim, when Moses prayed with his hands extended and God gave the victory to Joshua and his troops (Exod. 17). These Amalekites were nomads and Bedouins, fierce fighters of the desert, constantly on the move. The name given to the king, Eglon, may have been a taunting term of disdain; it means "fat bullock" in Hebrew, and as the story reaches its climax, the obesity of the king becomes apparent.

1. *Ehud's plot (3:15-25)*

Heroes often are unusual people, and Ehud was distinguished by being left-handed, an ironic state for a Benjamite whose name means "son of the right hand." His small sword, therefore, was over his right hip, whereas normally it would have been worn on his left side. Because it was hidden under his long, flowing garment, it completely escaped notice as he entered the king's palace. A sword of one cubit would probably have measured about eighteen inches, the length of the forearm with the extended fingers included.

The tribute would have been grain and produce, carried in baskets by Israelite attendants. After it had been offered to the Moabite overlords, Ehud dismissed his fellow servants in order to carry out his plan unassisted. First, he beguiled King Eglon with his hint of a secret message for his ears alone. Then he was invited to join the king in his "room of cooling," evidently an upper chamber with the private royal quarters behind double doors. Ehud approached the monarch as if to reveal his message, but quickly drew his sword, buried it with the hilt in the king's belly, and left him dying on the floor. Then he locked the doors behind him, casually walked out of the palace, and made his escape.

The servants waited too long, assuming that their monarch was occupied in his bathroom (literally "sitting on his feet," a common euphemism in Hebrew). When they finally unlocked the chamber doors, they discovered the body of their assassinated king on the floor.

2. *Ehud's victory (3:26-30)*

Meanwhile, Ehud fled back to his homeland, to Seirah, evidently a small town in Benjamin or Ephraim. Soon he had mustered a small army and engaged the Moabites in a surprise attack. The result was a great victory for Israel that brought freedom to the people and security along the Jordan River and the border with Moab. This time the land would enjoy rest for two generations, eighty years.

Ehud was considered worthy of high honor as a "savior" in Israel, yet no mention is made of the Spirit in his life. Such an act of treachery and violence would normally be condemned, except that the Moabite king had dealt wickedly with the Israelites, and his death was both a recompense for his evil deeds and a means of liberation for the tribes. Through the inspired mind of the prophet who wrote the book of Judges, we can watch the effects of sin. And the

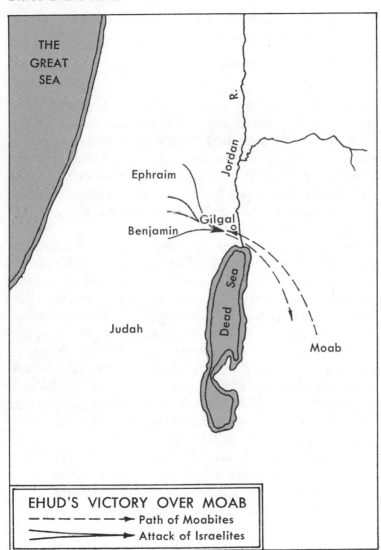

THE
GREAT
SEA

Ephraim

Jordan R.

Gilgal

Benjamin

Judah

Dead Sea

Moab

EHUD'S VICTORY OVER MOAB
— — — — — — ► Path of Moabites
————————► Attack of Israelites

New Testament confirms the outcome: "Whatever a man sows, this he will also reap" (Gal. 6:7*b*).

C. SHAMGAR, THE JUDGE (3:31)

Judah, however, was threatened from another direction, by the Philistines to the southwest (3:31). God sent Shamgar to put down the enemy and deliver His people. Shamgar's exploit of killing 600 Philistines with an oxgoad, or plowshare, an iron-tipped staff up to eight feet long (cf. 1 Sam. 13:21; Acts 9:5), is a foretaste of Samson's feat with the "jawbone of a donkey" (Judg. 15:15). Shamgar's foreign name and connection with Jael in the following chapter (5: 6) suggest that he was one of the Kenites.

The judge's name, Shamgar, has been found a number of times in the Nuzi Tablets from Mesopotamia, so it may not be a Hebrew name. This raises the question of his national identity: could he be a Canaanite and still serve God's purpose in delivering Israel? Certainly he was highly esteemed by the Israelites, as the song of Deborah and Barak verifies (5:6). A second problem is the mention of Anath, one of the Canaanite goddesses. Albright has pointed out that Anath was both the "virgin" sister of Baal and also his consort, at times portrayed in the form of a heifer. If Shamgar was indeed a worshiper of this pagan deity, his place in the book of Judges is hard to account for. There is another explanation, however, for his title, "Son of Anath." The phrase could mean that he was a native of the town called "Bethanoth," which was in the south (Josh. 15:59) and fits in with his exploits against the Philistines.

4

A PROPHETESS AND A GENERAL
LEAD GOD'S ARMY

D. DEBORAH AND BARAK AND THE CANAANITES
   (4:1—5:31)

APOSTASY RETURNED TO ISRAEL, and with it came the cycle of evil and oppression. This time the focus is upon the northern tribes, whom "The LORD sold . . . into the hand of Jabin king of Canaan, who reigned in Hazor" (4:2a). This powerful city had been conquered and burned by Joshua and his army not too many years before, yet the Canaanites were able to return and rebuild it. The victory of Joshua, as recorded in chapter 11 of his book, has various points in common with the battle in Judges 4 and 5, the most obvious being the king's name, Jabin. The two monarchs may have had a dynastic connection. Sisera was the military leader of the Canaanite confederation that had been oppressing the Israelites and now threatened to destroy them with 900 iron chariots.

1. *Deborah, the prophetess (4:1-5)*

Deborah's Hebrew name means "honeybee." She had earned the title of prophetess for her inspired words from God and her wisdom in arbitrating disputes between the

Israelites. Of all the judges, only Deborah was clearly engaged in the work of "judging" as we normally think of it.
The song in chapter 5 describes Deborah as "a mother in
Israel" (v. 7), meaning that a housewife was guiding the
nation. But it was her inward faith and power that inspired
Barak and his men to dare to meet their enemy on the battlefield.

The "court" where Deborah administered justice was a
certain date palm tree in the Ephraim hills between Ramah
and Bethel. Barak lived further to the north at Kedesh of
Naphtali, near Mount Tabor and to the east of the Valley
of Jezreel. Here the victory would be won over Sisera and
his Canaanite army. Esdraelon is another name for this
Plain of Megiddo where so many terrible wars had been
fought and would continue to be waged through the centuries.

2. *Barak, commander for God (4:6-16)*

Barak's demand that the prophetess accompany him in the
battle revealed his fear of the outcome and the weakness of
his faith. Deborah's presence was no more vital to insure
the Lord's support than the physical presence of the Ark of
the Covenant would be of any help later when Eli allowed
the sacred object to be taken out on the battlefield (1 Sam.
4:4). Barak probably assumed that the prediction in verse
9 referred to Deborah; but, as it turned out, a Kenite woman,
Jael received the glory that might have been his.

Nothing is mentioned in the prose account of chapter 4
about the miraculous way the Lord aided the Israelite tribes
in their victory over the Canaanites. Only in the song of
victory, chapter 5, do we learn that the forces of nature re-

sponded at the critical moment, engulfing the enemy in a downpour of rain and hail and miring down his chariot wheels so that the chariots were useless in the battle. Sisera and all his troops fled in confusion from the Plain of Esdraelon, with Barak and the Israelites in close pursuit. Harosheth-hagoyim, Sisera's kingdom, is the term for the general region of upper Galilee; it means literally "the woodlands of the nations," or perhaps "the lumber mills of the nations."

3. *Sisera, Canaanite general (4:17-24)*

The general of the Canaanites, Sisera, had slipped away in another direction and found shelter in the tent of a Kenite woman named Jael. At her overtures of kindness, the warrior stopped to rest in his flight. The woman showed excessive hospitality to her guest, offering milk and a comfortable bed and then agreeing to stand watch over him. But, as the general slept, Jael approached with a tent peg and mallet and pinned his head to the ground, killing him instantly. Barak ran up shortly thereafter to find his famous enemy already dead; the glory of victory was lost to him and given to a woman.

4. *Victory song of praise to God (5:1-31)*

Deborah's and Barak's song of victory is among the most beautiful poems of the Old Testament. Most critics acknowledge its antiquity, and all admire its vivid, dramatic, rhythmic style. Those unfamiliar with Semitic parallelism and poetry need to examine the second lines to detect their reflection of the theme ideas—sometimes amplifying, sometimes extending, or sometimes expressing the antithesis of the first line of the couplet.

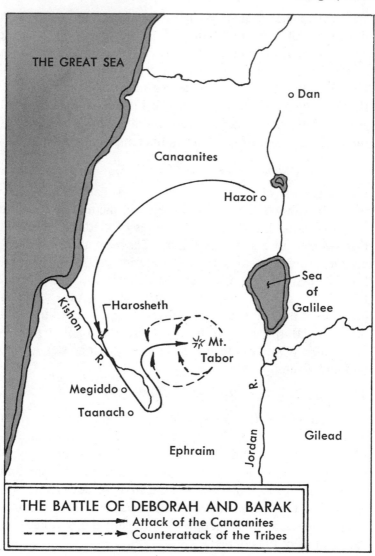

THE GREAT SEA

o Dan

Canaanites

Hazor o

Sea
of
Galilee

Harosheth

Kishon

R.

Mt.
Tabor

Megiddo o

Taanach o

Jordan

R.

Gilead

Ephraim

THE BATTLE OF DEBORAH AND BARAK

———→ Attack of the Canaanites

– – – –→ Counterattack of the Tribes

a. *Past deliverance contrasted with recent oppression (vv. 2-8).* The song begins with praises to the Lord for His great deeds during the Exodus and wilderness period of Israel's history (vv. 2-5). It then confesses the dire conditions that existed under the then-present oppression by the Canaanites of Hazor (vv. 6-8).

b. *Sounding the battle call (vv. 9-18).* Deborah and Barak mustered the tribes for battle, but some failed to respond (vv. 9-15a). The men of Reuben and Gad (Gilead) remained behind (vv. 15b-17a); Dan and Asher seemed not to notice the call to action (v. 17b). (Notice that the song viewed these latter tribes as seagoing peoples. As such, by that time they may have become too closely associated with their Phoenician and Canaanite neighbors to engage them in war.)

c. *The battle (vv. 19-23).* The scene of the battle is Taanach, "near the waters of Megiddo." Why is the imposing fortress of Megiddo not mentioned as the primary location? Because this battle happened during the twelfth century B.C., when Megiddo was in ruins; Megiddo remained weak until it was rebuilt by David and Solomon. Taanach was a major city near the Kishon stream, which is really too small to be classed as a river through this section of its course.

The Canaanites charged up into the Valley of Jezreel on their 900 chariots of iron. They invaded from the western side as the troops of Israel led by Barak came from the east (see 4:14). Normally, foot soldiers would have had no chance of defeating the war horses and charioteers from Hazor and the northern cities, but, in a moment, everything changed as a rainstorm flooded the valley. In confusion, the enemy soldiers had to abandon their chariots and run for safety. Most were cut down by Barak's warriors. Thus, the songsters cried out with glee, "The stars fought from heaven" (5:20). Divine intervention brought victory once again to the tribes. Here the account of victory is interrupted by a curse against the Israelites from the city of Meroz, site as yet unknown, for their cowardice in avoiding the battle (v. 23).

d. *Jael's part in winning the victory (vv. 24-27)*. Gratitude and admiration are profusely lavished upon Jael, wife of Heber the Kenite, for her brave deed in killing the enemy general. She is called the "most blessed . . . of women in the tent," a reference to the Bedouin life of the Kenites, many of whom preferred their tents and meanderings to the settled life of a farmer. Her tent peg may have been an iron spike, but the term equally fits the description of a narrow wooden peg. Sisera's death while asleep does not fit literally the scene described in verse 27. However, the death of a warrior is thought of as a fall, and the metaphoric language describes his death in slow motion: "Between her feet he bowed, he fell, he lay; between her feet he bowed, he fell; where he bowed, there he fell dead."

e. *Pathos of the fallen general (vv. 28-31)*. One final scene completes the victory song: the queen, mother of Sisera, is portrayed as peering from her window, waiting for her son to ride up as usual with the spoils of his triumph. But she waits in vain for a son who will never return.

These Canaanite forces from the northern cities were the last enemies from within Israel's borders to challenge her authority. Future nations would invade from the outside. Meanwhile, Deborah's and Barak's good leadership secured a long period of peace and prosperity.

5

MISSION IMPOSSIBLE

E. GIDEON AND THE MIDIANITES (6:1—8:28)

THE PERPETUAL BACKSLIDING of God's people is documented in the book of Judges. The prophet Jeremiah many years later exclaimed, "Has a [pagan] nation changed gods, when they were not gods? But My people have changed their glory for that which does not profit" (Jer. 2:11). This describes the early days of Gideon, when Baals and Ashtaroth were served and the Lord God forsaken. To punish His people, God sent in warlike tribes from the desert. The Amalekites, perpetual antagonists of Israel, swarmed in from the east and south, and the Midianites joined them, driving up with their herds and camels from the region near the Bay of Aqaba. The "sons of the east" (6:3) probably included some Edomites and Ammonites as well. As Bedouins and shepherds, they were interested in grain but not in the extensve farming of the Israelites, so the land's produce was largely destroyed (6:4). All animals of value were taken away with their own flocks (6:5). Camels were the special mark of the desert nomad and were feared for their prowess in battle.

In the Scriptures, we learn that the Midianites were half brothers to the Hebrews, Midian being a son of Abraham

through his last wife, Keturah (Gen. 25:1-6). Moses found
the Midianites hospitable, married Zipporah, the daughter of
the priest of Midian, and lived among them for forty years.
A close association also existed between the Midianites and
Moab, as is attested in Numbers 22:4. The Sinai evidently
was also part of the territory roamed freely by Midianites,
since Moses was at the sacred mountain in Sinai when the
Lord appeared in the burning bush. Thus, it is clear that
Midian's boundaries were not clearly marked and that its
people wandered or spread out over many parts of the area.

As the afflicted Israelites prayed and cried out to the Lord
for help, He sent a prophet to recall God's mighty works of
salvation that had made possible their Exodus from Egypt
and their possession of the promised land. But the people's
actions had not corresponded to the faithfulness of their God.
"You have not obeyed Me," God said through the prophet
(6:10). This was really the same message echoed by John
the Baptist, calling people to repentance (see Matt. 3:1-12).

Following these words from the unnamed prophet, the
"angel of the LORD" appeared to Gideon (6:12). Few
events are more wonderful or mysterious than the occasional
visits of the "angel of the LORD" in the Bible. Could this
heavenly visitor be the preincarnate Son of God, as some
have suggested? At times the Angel of the Lord was addressed as God, worshiped, and believed to be the divine
presence (Gen. 21:17; 22:11—the Angel spoke as God;
31:11, 13—the Angel claimed to be God, "The God of
Bethel"; Exod. 3:2—the Angel spoke from the burning bush
to Moses; 2 Sam. 24:16-17—the Angel sent a plague on the
people and was addressed as God). The New Testament ap-
pearances of "an angel of the Lord" are similar in kind and

purpose (Matt. 2:13, 19; Luke 1:11; Acts 5:19; 12:23). However, since "messenger" is a frequent nuance of the word for *angel,* it is also possible to conclude that the visitor was either a human spokesman for God or a member of the angelic hosts on a special mission from God. In this passage Gideon will address him as "Lord," using the Hebrew *adonai* (Judg. 6:15). But the context uses the sacred name, *Yahweh,* for the Angel in other places (6:14, 16, 23). Once he is called the "angel of God" (*elohim,* 6:20).[1]

Gideon was honored with the recognition that he was a "valiant warrior" (6:12). Rather than an allusion to past deeds of courage by Gideon, this title showed his status among the upper class of landowners and leaders in Israel.

Any farmer along the Mediterranean would find it ludicrous to see a man trying to do his threshing in a winepress. Since Gideon was no fool, we can be assured that the situation was highly critical. He normally would have used a flat place were the winds and open air would blow away the chaff, but he needed to hide his harvest from the eyes of the invaders. Thus, he was obliged to thresh his grain in the covered shelter where grapes were pressed into wine.

1. *Gideon's call (6:13-24)*

In response to the Angel's command to go forth and save Israel from the Midianites, Gideon said, "How shall I deliver Israel? Behold, my family is the least in Manasseh" (6:15a). The word for *family* is the usual term for "thousand" (*eleph*) in the original language, but it often carries the meaning required here of "family," or "clan" (cf. Mic. 5:2, where the Messiah was to come from one of the clans of Judah).

1. Robert G. Boling, *Judges,* The Anchor Bible (Garden City, N.Y.: Doubleday, 1975), p. 132.

It was proper to offer food to a guest, and the boiling of a lamb was the best meal that could be presented; it would take a few hours to prepare, but the Angel of the Lord waited for his host to get the meal ready and bring it back. Although the Lord said, "I will be with you," the words were not enough assurance for the cautious Israelite; Gideon wanted unmistakable proof that God would help him. This proof was provided in the breathtaking moment when the Angel of the Lord touched the meat and unleavened bread with the end of his staff and fire sprang up from the rock, consuming the food. Then the Angel vanished! The truth dawned upon Gideon that his guest had been truly supernatural, and he was seized by fear. Then he heard the Lord's voice, perhaps now from within, reassuring him that he would live with God's blessing on his life (6:23). Gideon built an altar there and named the place Yahweh-Shalom, "The LORD is Peace" (6:24).

2. *Victory at home (6:25-40)*

God's first test of Gideon was to clean up the pagan shrine in his home town. How often it is necessary for new believers to show their faith by some open witness to those nearest to them—their families, friends, and local churches. Gideon's mission to tear down the altar to Baal was no small task; the pagan shrine was awesome both for its size and for its legendary importance in the society of that day. Gideon went in by night with his father's bull calf and dragged off the great stones that formed the altar of the nonexistent rain-god of the Canaanites. He also pulled down the pole-symbols called Asherah, which may have been obscene images connected with the fertility cult of Astarte or Baal. Then he replaced the pagan shrine with a new altar to the Lord and made a true sacrifice with the second bull.

As one might expect, the local Baal-worshipers were furious and immediately searched for the person responsible for destroying their altar to Baal. When Gideon was found to be the guilty one, they marched on his house and demanded that he be turned over to them for execution. But Joash, Gideon's father, was ready for them with the retort, "If [Baal] is a god, let him contend for himself" (6:31). The crisis passed, and Gideon became a heroic figure bearing a new title: Jerubbaal, meaning "Let Baal plead his case." As the news of the dramatic events at Ophrah spread rapidly throughout the tribes, Gideon became a symbol for the true believers in the Lord, and many of the tribes began to rally around him.

The clause in 6:34, "So the Spirit of the LORD came upon Gideon," literally reads, "And the Spirit of the Lord clothed Himself with Gideon." Few metaphors better fit the "filling" of the servant of God for Spirit-inspired leadership than this one. All Christians are urged by the apostle Paul to allow the Holy Spirit to fill, that is, take possession completely of, their hearts and lives (Eph. 5:18). Many others in the early church experienced this filling (Acts 4:8, 31; 9:17; 13:52).

As further confirmation that the Lord would really deliver Israel through him, Gideon "put a fleece of wool on the threshing floor," and asked for another sign of God's power in his life (6:36-38). Gideon repeated his test, and again the Lord was merciful to His servant and answered his prayer (6:39-40). These were visible signs to reassure Gideon of God's will before the great battle. After the resurrection of Christ, a similar doubt existed in the mind of Thomas, who insisted on seeing the nailprints and touching the scars of the crucified Lord (John 2:24-25). It is significant, however, that Jesus said, "Blessed are they who did not see, and yet believed" (20:29*b*). It is better not to test God.

3. *Preparation for battle (7:1-15)*

Chapter 7 opens with the army of Israelites gathered for battle at the spring called Harod, a powerful, bubbling stream that emerges from the foot of Mount Gilboa and winds eastward through the Valley of Jezreel to the Jordan. We learn, however, from 6:35 that only four of the tribes were called upon to fight by Gideon's messengers: Manasseh, Asher, Zebulun, and Naphtali; the number that responded was 32,000.

But the Lord objected to this number and commanded Gideon to dismiss all who were afraid (7:1-3). It is not surprising that two-thirds left the scene to return to their homes. Gideon remained with only 10,000 men, a relatively small force compared to the vast army of the Midianites and Amalekites that was camped less than ten miles away.

Again the Lord objected to the size of Gideon's army. There would have to be a final test at the stream Harod, which was uncomfortably close to the camp of the Midianites. Gideon was instructed to disqualify all soldiers who "kneeled to drink." As a result, 9,700 men were ordered to return to their homes (lit. "places"). This kneeling position must have placed the thirsty men with their faces down at the surface of the water, because they did not lift it up with their hands to drink.

Only 300 out of 10,000 soldiers "licked the water with

their hands to their mouths" (7:6, literal translation). Evidently this smaller group brought the water up to their mouths in their hands while taking a more upright position on their knees. "Lapping as a dog laps" is the phrase that has raised the most discussion, because it suggests that one has lowered his face near the water and fits the position taken by the 9,700 who were disqualified. Yet, "lapping" is also possible from water cupped in the hand, and this is the position of the 300 who were chosen. There is still room for argument about the significance of the two positions, but it is best to assume that the 9,700 were showing careless indifference to the enemy nearby and that the 300 remained more alert and ready for the conflict.

Gideon's nocturnal mission to the edge of the enemy camp was foolhardy from a human point of view, but the Lord led and protected him; he would receive additional proof of the supernatural power of God controlling all events of his life. What an awesome sight met his eyes, a sea of tents that stretched across the valley and around the base of Mount Moreh! With his armorbearer, Purah, Gideon approached close enough to overhear a conversation between two enemy soldiers about a strange dream. One had seen in his sleep a barley cake roll into the camp and strike down a tent of Midian. It was absurd! Cakes of barley were small and of the lowest quality, eaten only by the very poor and destitute. Then the truth dawned upon them. The barley cake represented none other than Gideon, leader of the afflicted Israelites. They had heard of Gideon's miraculous powers and favor with God and were afraid of him. God allowed Gideon to hear confirmation of his impending victory from the mouth of the enemy.

4. *Gideon's great victory (7:16-22)*

The attack was carefully planned. First, the band of 300 was subdivided into three companies, a common tactic in the ancient world (see 1 Sam. 11:11; 2 Sam. 18:2; Job 1:17). An earthen jar (collected in advance from the main body of Israelites before they were sent home) was distributed to every man, and then a torch was hidden within each jar, where its light would not show until the signal was given. Trumpets, evidently of rams' horns, were parceled out, and the orders were given to surround the camp of Midian, wait for the signal, and then break the jars and wave the torches together. Each would shout the battle cry "For the Lord and for Gideon!" as he blew his trumpet (7:18).

"At the beginning of the middle watch" (7:19) would have been shortly after 10 P.M., since the night was divided into three periods of four hours each, starting at 6 P.M. The newly posted guards had just arrived at their posts and were not as yet accustomed to the darkness. Torches used in that period probably were faggots of wood dipped in resin or tar; they would smolder inside the jar, and then as the torches were waved through the air, their embers would burst into flame.

The attack happened exactly as planned, creating total panic and confusion among the Midianites. They imagined that every trumpeter led a full troop of soldiers and that these bands were coming in from all sides. In the sudden tumult and flurry of attempts to escape, many enemy soldiers killed each other. The "barley cake" of the dream had indeed rolled over the tents of Midian!

It is significant that no mention is made of swords or weapons in the hands of Gideon's band of 300. "Each stood in his place" (7:21), trusting the Lord to fulfill His promise and win the battle for Israel. Every believer, when facing a difficult problem, needs to learn this lesson of waiting for the Lord's answer and victory, rather than trying to force some solution abortively in his own strength. David never lifted up his hand against the Lord's "anointed," even though King Saul was his personal enemy and was seeking his life. May the Lord give us courage and faith such as this.

5. *The retreat of the enemy (7:23—8:21)*

In the description of the flight of the Midianites, only a few of the place names can be clearly identified. They retreated eastward toward the Jordan Valley and the desert beyond. Beth-shittah may have been the modern Arab town of Shattan near Bethshan. Zererah sounds like the Jordan Valley town of Zarethan (1 Kings 7:46). Succoth and Penuel were on the east bank, near the Jabbok River where it flows into the Jordan.

Oreb and Zeeb, meaning "raven" and "wolf," had names typical of desert nomads to this day. They were princes that represented the twin kings of Midian, Zebah and Zalmunna, probably from the two leading clans of the nation. This was an ancient "balance of power" arrangement, fairly common to the people of the Near East, that circumvented the despotism of one absolute monarch.

Ephraimites arrived in time to take revenge upon these chieftains of Midian (7:24-25). However, they were not happy to have been involved merely in the "mopping up" exercises. They blamed Gideon and criticized him severely for failing to give them a part in the initial battle (8:1). This, of course, was precisely the arrogant spirit that the Lord had determined not to allow the men who participated in the battle to have. The greater part of Gideon's army had been

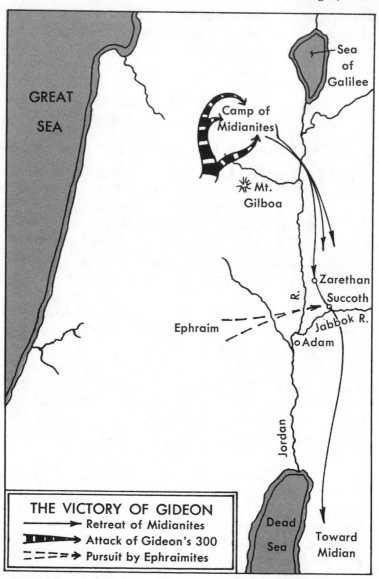

THE VICTORY OF GIDEON
→ Retreat of Midianites
▬▬▶ Attack of Gideon's 300
--- --→ Pursuit by Ephraimites

disqualified because the victory was not to be won by man-power but by the miracle-working Lord of all nations. Gideon replied to these complaints with restraint. He commended the Ephraimites for their mighty works, far greater than his own, which is the meaning of the proverb about the grapes in verse 8:2. Tactfully, he soothed their feelings and preserved the unity of the tribes. Later on, when a very similar disagreement arose between Jephthah and the Ephraimites (chap. 12), Jephthah took a tougher approach, but this lack of tact brought on a tragic civil war between the other tribes and Ephraim.

Local inhabitants in the Jordan Valley were invited to co-operate with Gideon; bread was urgently lacking for the tired and hungry soldiers. However, the citizens of the towns of Succoth and Penuel refused to meet this moderate request (8:6, 8). Gideon promised to punish them when he had vanquished the Midian troops still fleeing from the battle. This he returned to do, using thorns and briars in the discipline of the elders of Succoth (8:15-16). At Penuel, Gideon broke down the tower and executed the men.

Linguists have shown great interest in the lad from Succoth who was able to write down the names of seventy-seven elders of his city (8:14). What language did he know? Could all citizens read and write in those days? The alphabetic script of Canaan had only twenty-two letters and was in use by the middle of the second millennium, attested in the Sinai; Semitic writing may be seen in the turquoise mines of the Egyptians, where slaves from Canaan left their markings.[2]

Gideon's act of judgment against the two kings came in answer to their horrendous crime of killing his brothers at

2. William F. Albright, *The Archaeology of Palestine*, rev. ed. (Harmondsworth, Eng.: Penguin, 1960), p. 189. The Sinaitic script is included on the chart of alphabets, p. 192.

Tabor (8:18-19). This previous deed is not mentioned in
the account of the battle; it may have taken place shortly before or during the flight, when local skirmishes were likely to
have taken place. Gideon's sense of justice, however, was
not shared by his first-born son, Jether. Overcome with fear,
the young man drew back from killing the two Midianite
kings, so Gideon performed the deed himself. "Crescents" of
gold or silver ornaments were confiscated from the necks of
the camels of the two kings. The term in Hebrew means
"little moons, good luck charms usually dedicated to the
Semitic moon-god." Such ornaments still grace the animals
of the Arab nomads and symbolize their ancestral home in
the fertile crescent of the Near East.

6. *Keeping the peace (8:22-35)*

The Israelites had defeated their great foe and oppressor.
Now they cheered Gideon's name and power and sought to
make him their king. How quickly is the work of God forgotten! "The men of Israel said to Gideon, 'Rule over us,
both you and your son, also your son's son, for you have delivered us from the hand of Midian' " (8:22). No more noble
act of this hero-judge can be found than Gideon's refusal to
accept the authority offered to him. He sensed that God's
power was not dynastic or transferrable to his children in a
royal line. "The LORD shall rule over you," was his reply
(8:23b). God would raise up a series of prophets and judges
with God-given power and led by the Holy Spirit to rule His
people. The great prophet Samuel showed similar feelings
against monarchical rule when he warned against putting a
king over the tribes (1 Sam. 8:4-9).

How can a man act so nobly as to refuse a kingship in

order to exalt God, then immediately afterward commit an act of blasphemy against Him? Peter at Caesarea Philippi did something akin to this. First he spoke for God as he confessed Christ; then he spoke for Satan as he rebuked Christ (see Matt. 16:15-23). There is grave danger that all of us will be inconsistent in our witness. It can be argued that Gideon really had the best of intentions when he requested the golden earrings and crescents and formed an "ephod" to preserve the memory of the Lord's mighty power in delivering His people from the Midianites. An ephod, a garment normally worn by the high priest, was beautifully decorated with jewels, as symbols of the twelve tribes of Israel. It also contained the sacred stones, the "Urim and the Thummim" (Lev. 8:8). But Gideon's ephod is difficult to imagine as a garment, since it was molded from gold, set up on display, and decked with ornaments. Some consider it to have been an idol, but there is no evidence of the worship of the Baals until after the death of Gideon (cf. 8:33).

Gideon's intentions evidently were to exalt the Lord God with a memorial in his hometown, possibly on the altar he himself had erected in his first mission for God. However, the thing "became a snare to Gideon and his household" (8:27), meaning that it led them astray and cost them the honor and original popularity so well deserved by Gideon's victories. One suggestion for this is that the true priests would have resided at Shiloh, the resting place of the tabernacle. Any competing center for worship would have been a threat to their ministry, especially if it involved further transgression of the laws and regulations for sacrifices given by Moses. If the tribes neglected Shiloh to worship the Lord at Gideon's ephod, this alone would justify the condemnation recorded in 8:27.

6

TREACHERY IN ISRAEL

F. ABIMELECH'S TREACHERY (9:1-57)

GIDEON TOOK MANY WIVES and raised a family of seventy
sons. (Daughters were never counted in the genealogies of
the Hebrews.) Such action was typical of the ancient kings
of Palestine, who sought to maintain their authority through
their progeny. Perhaps the great hero, for all his disclaimers,
was guilty of acting as if he were a king. Certainly this multi-
plication of wives was another weakness in Gideon for which
his family would suffer bitterly. God had warned future
kings, through the Law, against taking many wives (Deut.
17:17). Gideon's marriage to a concubine, a secondary
status of wife in Israel, resulted in the birth of a wicked son,
Abimelech. The concubine came from the city of Shechem,
notorious for its violent, lawless citizens. When Abimelech
received his name meaning "my father is a king," the impli-
cation is strong that his mother's family intended to take ad-
vantage of Gideon's fame and authority and seek to transfer
Gideon's power to their relative.

1. *Abimelech's evil plot (9:1-6)*

As Abimelech grew up, he began to plot the seizure of
power from his brothers and the promotion of himself to the

role of king among the central tribes. He gained the support of the men of Shechem, even receiving a gift of seventy pieces of silver from the shrine of Baal-berith in the city. Abimelech cajoled the people, saying, "Remember that I am your bone and your flesh" (9:2*b*—the Hebrew idiom for one of the same family, cf. Gen. 2:23; 29:14; 2 Sam. 5:1; 19:12). Thus, Abimelech persuaded the mixed population of Shechem to follow him in the raid against his brothers at Ophrah, where he murdered seventy of them on a single stone (9:5). This site may have been Gideon's old altar in the center of the town.

By this evil act, Abimelech became the undisputed leader of the Shechemites, and they immediately made him their king. At the coronation rites, two parts of the city could be discerned—the average citizens of Shechem and the people from the "Beth-millo," evidently the noble families, since the millo was an inner fortification, or tower. The coronation took place under the old sacred tree, the "terebinth" that carried memories dating back to the patriarchs (Gen. 12:6; 35:4) and also to the renewal of the covenant under Joshua (Josh. 24:26). The passage in Joshua refers to a "great stone" under the tree of Shechem, which some have identified with this pillar where Abimelech was crowned. Modern visitors at the archaeological site of ancient Shechem will notice the remains of an imposing stone or pillar within the confines of the temple area, suggesting the kind of stone this might have been.

2. *Jotham's fable (9:7-21)*

Meanwhile, Jotham, Gideon's youngest son and the only one who escaped the slaughter by Abimelech, daringly ap-

proached the edge of the city of Shechem and challenged the
people to reconsider their choice of a king. He stood on the
"top of Mount Gerizim," actually on one of the lower ledges
of the mountain, in order to be heard within the walls of the
city.

Jotham's fable of the trees, among the most famous fables
in all literature, dealt with the political crisis caused by a
corrupt leader. The trees discussed together their need for a
king to rule over them, then extended an invitation to the
oldest of the trees, the olive, which refused, as did the fig
tree and the vine (9:8-13). A note of scorn can be detected
in these replies that left the rest of the trees in a somewhat
pathetic as well as desperate situation. It is significant that
the fable used the term "anoint" for the act of kingship, since
it is from this same word that *Messiah* is derived. The offer
of the kingdom to the "bramblebush" was an obvious slur on
the character of Abimelech (9:14). This plant belongs to
the thorn-scrub bushes of the steppe areas of Palestine; it has
no fruit and very meager shade. So the "buckthorn" accepted
the clamor of the trees for a king, provided they would all
agree to the ludicrous idea of taking refuge in its shade!
(9:15). The final line of the fable is prophetic: fire would
indeed result from the evil work and leadership of Abimelech.
Frequently in the Scriptures fire is used as a symbol for war
and divine judgment, as it is here in the prediction of Shechem's fate. However, fire in the literal sense is frequently
connected with the buckthorn or bramblebush, since it was
used as kindling in cook fires (Exod. 22:6; Psalm 58:9;
Eccles. 7:6).

Jotham concluded his speech with words of biting sarcasm:
"If you have treated the house of Gideon with sincerity and

truth, and properly honored him for all of his heroic deeds
on your behalf, then be glad in your choice of Abimelech.
But if you have not been good and true to Gideon's memory,
may all of you be destroyed! May Abimelech consume you,
and you consume him!" (7:15-20, author's trans.). The force
of these final statements is that of a curse upon Abimelech
and the men of Shechem. Jotham had to run for his life and
hide from the anger of his brother (9:21).

3. *Abimelech's troubled reign (9:22-49)*

"Now Abimelech ruled over Israel three years" (9:22).
This does not mean that he was actually a king; the term is
closer to the idea of governor. Nor does "Israel" imply all
twelve tribes in this context. Abimelech's power probably
did not extend beyond the central areas of Ephraim and Manasseh. Those were years of trouble and treachery, for the
Lord sent "an evil spirit" to create strife between Abimelech
and his subjects (9:23). A similar expression tells what happened to King Saul in his fits of anger against David (1 Sam.
16:14). We read also that a "deceiving spirit" was sent by
God into false prophets of King Ahab to entice him into a
decision to go to war and be killed (1 Kings 22:19-23).
One could, therefore, interpret this "evil spirit" as a demonic
angel under the Lord's command. But evil (Hebrew *ra'*) in
its basic nuance refers to a disaster or calamity. When God
sends *evil,* it is always an intervening force of moral and
righteous judgment, corresponding to the wickedness of the
situation.

The climax of the story shows how the Lord dealt in history
with many who dared to transgress His moral laws. Abimelech had taken up residence at a fortress five miles south-

east of Shechem, a town called Arumah (the same called Tormah in the Hebrew text of 9:41). He placed Zebul, one of his officials, in charge of Shechem, and Zebul relayed to Abimelech the news of the insurrection being plotted against him (9:30-31). A new leader of the non-Hebraic elements had appeared to challenge the authority of Abimelech at Shechem (9:24-29). The men were turning to this Gaal who poisoned their minds against Abimelech and armed them for a seditious move to take over his power. Then Gaal made a fatal mistake. Taking the advice of deceitful Zebul, he marched his forces outside the safety of Shechem's walls to attack Abimelech's army. The rebel force was wiped out. Angry because of the treachery of the Shechemites, Abimelech turned on the city that had shown him so many favors and completely leveled it, killing all of its citizens, including the families that lived within the *Beth-millo*, "the house of the fortress" (9:42-49).

Archaeologists date this terrible destruction of Shechem in the twelfth century B.C. and suggest that the *Beth-millo* may have been the temple area that was constructed over the highest part of the city.[1]

4. *Abimelech's death (9:50-57)*

Fires of war had consumed the Shechemites; now it would consume Abimelech himself. His death came at the moment of his apparent triumph and by the hand of a woman. At Thebez, he was about to destroy the last remnant of his enemies, who had gathered at the fortress of the city, when a woman threw down a stone that crushed his skull. His armorbearer finished him off, but a woman caused his death with the

1. Yohanan Aharoni, *The Land of the Bible: A Historical Geography* (Philadelphia: Westminster, 1967), p. 242.

"upper millstone," a heavy, cylinder-shaped stone about a foot long and several inches thick (9:53-54). "Thus God repaid the wickedness of Abimelech" (9:56) simply means that the Lord turned back his evil deeds upon himself; he "reaped what he sowed" in his life of violence and excessive ambition. All who joined him suffered the same destiny, which is a warning to men everywhere never to follow such a leader, least of all to permit him to rule as a king.

G. Two minor judges (10:1-5)

Two judges of Israel are now presented in brief review. Tola came from the northern tribe of Issachar, but he lived and ministered in the hills of Ephraim for twenty-three years (see Gen. 46:13). Since no one particular enemy is mentioned, his concern may have been to "save" the tribes from the inroads of heathen worship and idolatry (10:1-2).

Jair had a name that linked him with the early fathers of the tribe of Manasseh who settled on the east side of the Jordan (see Num. 32:41). His area of influence, like Jephthah's, was in the region of Gilead and north of the Jabbok River. This Jair was noted for his sizable family; he had thirty sons equipped with thirty asses, a sign in those days of wealth and status among the upper class (10:4). His thirty cities may not have been permanently built towns; their name, *Havvoth,* means a tent village. Still, their existence was clearly known at the time of the sacred writer of Judges, which may have been during the early years of King Saul (see "Introduction," p. 15).

7

MISGUIDED LEADER

H. JEPHTHAH AND THE AMMONITES (10:6—12:7)

ONCE AGAIN A FAMILIAR PHRASE introduces a new cycle of
events and a new judge in Israel. "Then the sons of Israel
again did evil in the sight of the LORD" (10:6a). The state of
apostasy is described here in greater detail than before, with
the gods of the neighboring peoples whom the Israelites worshiped when they forsook the Lord being listed. Such local
deities have been labeled "watchdog" gods, as each was believed to guard and favor its own particular territory. The
Sidonians of Phoenicia worshiped *Baal* and *Astarte,* the
"queen of heaven." In Syria it was probably the god *Tham-
muz,* although some bowed to the star-deity, *Athtar.* For the
Moabites it was the evil god *Chemosh,* whose idol was used
in the burning of child sacrifices (1 Kings 11:33). The
Philistines built their main temple to the grain-god called
Dagon, but they also worshiped *Baal-zebub* (2 Kings 1:2,
literally "lord of the flies," a metaphor for demons).[1]

With the Israelites trying to honor all of the false idols of
their neighbors, it is no wonder that the true God of the
heavens was angry with them (10:7). Monotheism is the

---

1. *Zabub* usually signified "flies" when used in a literal sense, but it also became a metaphor for "demons." See Cyrus Gordon, *Greek and Hebrew
Civilization* (New York: Norton, 1965), p. 246.

belief that there is no more to any other "god" than its visible stone or wood or metal image. Whereas the ancients assumed that the real spirits existed above the clouds and in the nature powers, such as the storm and the sea, the Hebrews believed there was nothing out there except the Creator-God and His angelic messengers.

The expression for *anger* in the Old Testament comes from a figure of speech meaning one's "nose is burning." Often the phrase is translated "His anger was kindled," an attempt to preserve at least a part of the figure. Such anthropomorphic descriptions of the Lord, who is pure spirit, only demonstrate how real He was as a personal being to the inspired writers of Scripture.

God turned the Israelites over to their enemies for a time of affliction to teach them a lesson as well as to punish them (10:7-8). The two and one-half tribes that had settled in Transjordan suffered the most, since the nearby Ammonites repeatedly devastated their lands. But even the tribes of Judah, Ephraim, and Benjamin were hard hit by these same bands of invaders from the desert (10:9).

Predictions of divine judgment in the Bible are often presented in an incomplete form, giving the impression that the doom is sealed and no way of recovery is possible. Such is the first conclusion one might reach from the Lord's statement to the afflicted Israelites when they begged Him for help: "I will deliver you no more" (10:13). God might have added the other half of the truth, "That is . . . unless you confess your sins and return in faith to Me." It was the same with Jonah's warning to the citizens of Nineveh: "Yet forty days and Nineveh will be overthrown" (Jonah 3:4*b*). Yet the Lord of love and mercy heard the Ninevites' cries of remorse and "relented concerning the calamity" He had threatened to do to them. Here, under the heavy hand of the Ammonites, the tribes of Israel began to pray for grace and confess their wrongdoings. Moreover, they acted upon their faith by putting away all of the foreign idols in their midst in order to serve the Lord (10:10-16). So the God of compassion extended help to the Israelites and directed His indignation toward their enemies.

1. *Jephthah's call and military strategy (11:1-29, 32-33)*

The life of Jephthah reads something like that of a hero out of a Greek play. From birth he suffered an unusual amount of pain and hardship. His mother had been a harlot; so, when his half brothers began to resent his presence, they threw him out of the house and denied him any inheritance (11:1-3). Their father's name was Gilead, just like the name of that region and the name of their early forefather, Gilead, son of Machir (1 Chron. 7:14). It was a normal practice to send away such illegitimate children, cruel as it now appears to us. Even Abraham drove away the sons of his other wives and made them founders of other nations, so they would not share in Isaac's inheritance (Gen. 21:10; 25:6).

Jephthah wandered away and joined a company of ruthless bandits in the "land of Tob," to the east and north of Gilead.[2] He acquired the skills of a fighter and became notorious for his ability to wage war. It was this reputation that brought him to mind when the tribes desperately needed a leader against the Ammonites. The elders, ruling fathers of the clans in Gilead, including his own brothers, called him back to lead a military campaign against Ammon.

2. George Adam Smith, *The Historical Geography of the Holy Land,* 25th ed. rev. (New York: Harper & Row, 1966), p. 393.

Jephthah's reply expressed the bitterness carried over from his youth as he reminded them of their hatred for him. Yet he did accept their invitation on condition that they would follow him and make him in reality their "head." The term is *rosh,* the most common word for a chief or prince, the one to whom first place is given in the line of authority. Genesis 1:1 has this same word, and there the meaning is "at the head of," or "in the beginning."

Few leaders in the Old Testament show more intelligence than Jephthah. His military strategy was comparable to that of Gideon and David. He knew the history of the tribes and the details of their lives during the Exodus and their invasion of Canaan, as his defense of Israel's claims to the disputed territories plainly revealed (11:15-27). He proved to the king of the Ammonites that the land had been properly taken in war from the Amorites led by Sihon and Og after all attempts to find a peaceful settlement had been frustrated. The Ammonites had no such early claim as this. And so for "three hundred years" the tribes of Reuben, Gad, and one-half of Manasseh had lived in Gilead and north of Moab.

This period of three hundred years between the death of Moses and the campaigns of Jephthah is difficult to harmonize with the genealogies of the tribes, in which only seven or eight generations are mentioned. Of course it could represent a round number taken as the sum of seven forties, forty being a round number for one generation. It is clear from a careful study of the names that gaps occur, and some overlapping needs to be assumed to make the data fit together smoothly.

2. *Jephthah's terrible vow (11:30-31, 34-40)*

Jephthah tried to be a servant of the Lord God of Israel,

but his actions revealed a tragic mixture of truth and error. His rash and foolish vow to offer to God the first person from his household who met him after the battle was like a fatal flaw in his character. On the one hand, he stood "before the LORD" during his appointment as head of the tribes at Mizpah (possibly a site in Gilead, rather than the better known Mizpah in Benjamin). When he undertook the battle, we read that the "Spirit of the LORD came upon" him (11:29). But only his pagan concepts could have prompted him to offer a human sacrifice for the victory and to utter a formal vow to that end (11:30-31). Certainly he was ignorant of the expressed sanctions of the Law of Moses against all child sacrifices (Lev. 18:21; 20:2-5; Deut. 12:29-31).

It would be hard to overestimate the fearful strength of a vow, taken publicly with witnesses, in the world of the ancient Hebrews. Later on, King Saul thought that he had to follow through with the execution of his own son, Jonathan, because of a similar rash vow he had made (1 Sam. 14:24, 44). Fortunately, the people rescued Jonathan from Saul because he had just won a great victory for Israel (1 Sam. 14:45).

The kind of vow that superseded all others in gravity was the one that promised to give something to God in sacrifice; it was called a *cherem,* which stood for an animal or gift totally and irredeemably committed to God (Lev. 27:28). Never for a moment did either the father, Jephthah, or the daughter consider anything but the fulfillment of the vow that they linked to the victory God had given (11:35-36).

It is only fair that we judge the actions of Jephthah within his own customs and times; yet, from every angle, he stands condemned. At best, he was ignorant of the divine will of

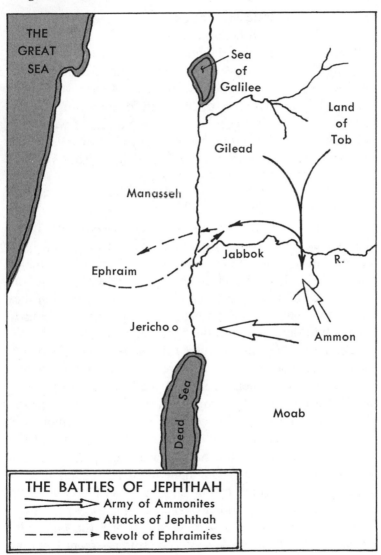

THE GREAT SEA

Sea of Galilee

Land of Tob

Gilead

Manasseh

Ephraim

Jabbok

R.

Jericho o

Ammon

Dead Sea

Moab

THE BATTLES OF JEPHTHAH

⟶ Army of Ammonites

⟶ Attacks of Jephthah

--→ Revolt of Ephraimites

God and the Mosaic laws against human sacrifices. Some have tried to alter the plain reading of the passage to mean that he merely sent his daughter away to live in perpetual virginity (11:37-38). But it is evident that the horrendous deed was indeed carried out at the end of the two months requested by the daughter of Jephthah for mourning the loss of motherhood. To the following generations of women in Israel, this heroic daughter became a symbol of loyalty and obedience; year after year they gathered to bewail her tragic end on the hills of Gilead (11:39-40).

3. *War with Ephraim (12:1-7)*

The tribe of Ephraim was easily offended whenever its influence was ignored or its dominant position was challenged. The men of Ephraim had been angered before, when Gideon did not invite them to join in his surpirse attack on the camp of the Midianites (8:1-3). Now, in a similar situation they turned their anger on Jephthah, accusing him of failing to call them in time to join in the fight against Ammon (12:1).

Jephthah lacked the tempered diplomacy of Gideon. He rebuked them severely for their refusal to come to his aid. "Where were you when we needed you?" is the substance of his retort (12:2). "I took my life in my hands," is a declaration of the high risk he took when he attacked the Ammonites with smaller forces (12:3). He said, "The LORD gave them into my hand. Why then have you come up . . . to fight against me?" (12:3*b*). But fight it out they did, brother against brother, demonstrating how the sins of envy and self-interest lead to strife and division (12:4).

In the battle that followed, Jephthah and the Gileadites scored another decisive victory. The soldiers from Ephraim tried to escape across the Jordan River to the safety of their homeland. However, they were challenged at the fords to identify themselves by repeating the word for "ear of corn"; in Hebrew, *shibboleth* (12:6). Local dialects had developed among the tribes, and the fleeing Ephraimites found it difficult to pronounce the letter *Shin* in the manner of the Gileadites; they said *sibboleth* instead. Caught by their own tongue, forty-two thousand were slain on the spot. It is legitimate to translate this number as "forty-two military contingents" since the term *eleph,* meaning "thousand," may also represent units or clans (cf. 6:15, where the same word refers to the clan of Gideon).

The size of Ephraim was no indication of the tribe's importance. When a census was taken a year after the Exodus from Egypt, Ephraim's men over twenty-one numbered 40,500 (Num. 1:33), but at the close of the forty years of desert wanderings, they were down to 32,500 (Num. 26:37). This made Ephraim the smallest of the tribes, except for Simeon, at the time of the entry into Canaan. A great future, however, had been marked out for Ephraim by the prophetic words of Jacob. As he blessed his twin grandsons, he crossed his hands and placed his right palm on Ephraim's head, proclaiming that Ephraim would be the greater: "His descendants shall become a multitude of nations" (Gen. 48:19*b*). But the grandeur of the tribe of Ephraim was slow in coming. The urge to lead was there, fed by a high self-esteem and a conviction of superiority above the others, but for many generations the bulk of the tribes paid no heed to Ephraim's claims. Her opportunity finally came after the downfall of Solomon's "Golden Age," when Jeroboam successfully led a revolt against Judah and the household of David. Ephraim became the central tribe of the northern federation, and Samaria was her great capital. The name of Ephraim was practically synonymous with that of Israel for two hundred years. The tribe retained its leadership until the fall of Samaria in 721 B.C. under the Assyrians.

Must there be an order of superiority or rank in every community? Christ taught His disciples not to call anyone "Rabbi," or "father," but to treat each other as brothers (Matt. 23:8-9). Again the example of the judges for us today is a negative one. We must learn never to act in envy or arrogance or to do anything at the expense of our brothers and neighbors. Conflict with tragic results usually follows such aggressive behavior.

I. THREE MINOR JUDGES (12:8-15)

Jewish tradition has linked the judge Ibzan with the name of Boaz, husband of Ruth and forefather of King David. Also in favor of this identification is a word from Josephus that this Bethlehem of Ibzan (12:8) is the Bethlehem of Judah.[3] However, the size of Ibzan's family, "thirty sons, and thirty daughters," would have required him to have had multiple wives as well as strong political power, which is incongruous with the life of Boaz as presented in the book of Ruth. A more likely suggestion is that Ibzan lived in northern Zebulun, where another Bethlehem existed about seven miles west of Nazareth.

The next judge, Elon, would have been Ibzan's neighbor if not his successor, since, he, too, was a Zebulunite. After eight years Elon died and was buried in Aijalon, a variation

3. Max Seligsohn, "Ibzan," in *The Jewish Encyclopaedia,* ed. Isidore Singer, 12 vols. (1901-5; reprint ed., New York: Ktav, 1964), 6:554.

of the same name. This Aijalon is also located in Galilee and is not to be confused with the valley where the "sun stood still" for Joshua, enabling him to win a great battle against the southern kings (Josh. 10:12).

The third minor judge in this passage is Abdon, whose name meant "service" or "servant." In Ephraim, where he lived and ruled over the central tribes, Abdon was known as the "Pirathonite" after his small village of Pirathon, perhaps modern Farata, which is just south of Nablus. Again we find a judge whose fame is measured by the size of his family. "Forty sons and thirty grandsons" would have put him ahead of Jair in fame and strength and made him equal to Gideon.

Little detail is recorded of life in Israel during the twenty-five years these three judges served, but it is evident that they succeeded in keeping the peace. A special place of honor was given to them in the chronicles of the tribes.

8

TARNISHED HERO

J. SAMSON AND THE PHILISTINES (13:1—16:31)

THE SCENE SHIFTS now to the western flank of Judah, where
the troublesome Philistines had grown strong enough to oppress their Israelite neighbors for a generation. The Bible
records the land of Caphtor as the former home of the Philistines (Deut. 2:23; Jer. 47:4; Amos 9:7; in Gen. 10:14, the
additional name of Casluhim is linked to their origin). This
means that the Philistines were Greek in background and
culture. We know from Egyptian records that these same
Philistines had invaded the delta and were subsequently
driven into Canaan by the armies of Ramses III about 1200
B.C. Aegean-type pottery has been discovered by archaeologists in the ruins of the cities of Philistia, and the character-
istics of the Philistines, as portrayed on the war scenes of
Egypt, bear close resemblance to the Minoans of Crete.[1]

The years of affliction under the Philistines, like the previous oppressions by other nations, were God's doing (13:1).
The Hebrew tribes grew cold in their faith and loyalty to God,
turning to corrupt and idolatrous Canaanite customs. Therefore, the divine Sovereign "gave them" into subjection to the
Philistines. All believers today must live in the awareness of

1. Robert G. Boling, *Judges,* The Anchor Bible (Garden City, N.Y.: Doubleday, 1975), p. 219.

this other side of the love of God—His concern to teach us the awfulness of sin, even when it means we must suffer to learn the lesson. The wise man of Proverbs said, "For whom the LORD loves He reproves" (3:12*a*); here is a warning for all of us.

1. *The endowed child (13:1-25)*

The birth of Samson paralleled that of Isaac, Samuel, John the Baptist, and our Lord Himself. An angel announced Samson's birth before his conception and instructed his father, Manoah, and his mother in how to ready their son for God's service. Strict observance of the Nazirite rules of sobriety was enjoined by the heavenly messenger. Both wine and strong drink were disallowed to mother and child, and Samson's hair was never to be cut so long as he lived, as a symbol of the favor of God (13:3-5). Children are a gift from God in more than the general sense of nature's bestowments, such as the rain, sunlight, air, and water. Every new life is a unique miracle directly from the hands of God. The father's "seed" can have no effect apart from the will and lifegiving power of the Lord. Samson's mother felt the same joy as did Sarah, Rebekah, Rachel, Hannah, Elizabeth, and Mary at their wonderous news. She was not surprised that the child was destined to be a special servant of Yahweh. She also understood why she herself was required to refrain from drinking strong drink or eating unclean foods while she carried that child. If he was to be "a Nazirite . . . from the womb," then he must never be contaminated with or come near to such items as those.

From this passage in Judges it is clear that the laws of purity were known and practiced before the settlement in

Canaan. It gives credence to the Mosaic legislation on the "clean and the unclean," dating back to the Sinai (Lev. 11). Wine and strong drink may have been denied to the Nazirite because of its connection with merrymaking and frivolity or because it was fermented and a symbol of corruption. The term in Hebrew for strong drink was *shakar,* and since they knew nothing of distilled spirits, it was either a heavy mixture of wines or the beer of the ancients made from grain. Philistines were especially fond of beer and drank it in their ritual feasts to Dagon, the grain-god. Beer mugs and flasks in copious numbers have been found by archaeologists in the sites of Philistine cities from Iron Age I, easily identified by their small holes that form a strainer for the dregs.

Nazirites in Israel were usually men of deep religious feeling who kept solemn vows for the service of Yahweh. The three main vows are listed in Numbers 6 as follows: a Nazirite may not cut his hair, drink any wine whatsoever, or come in contact with a dead body (usually extended to all the *kosher* laws). Most Nazirites took these vows for a limited period of six months to a year, but a few became so dedicated that they kept them for their entire lives. As in this case of Samson's parents, Hannah offered her son to the Lord as a Nazirite for "as long as he lives" (1 Sam. 1:22, 28). The life-style of John the Baptist suggests that he, too, was a lifetime Nazirite, dedicated to God by his parents before he was born (Luke 1:13-15).

2. *The angelic visitor (13:3-5, 9-20)*

Who was the messenger that came to Samson's parents, announcing Samson's future birth—man, God, or angel? The parent's first impressions were evidently of a human prophet, a "man of God" (13:6, 8). A good case could be built in favor of this interpretation, since prophets have been sent on similar missions, then snatched away when the message was delivered. However, Manoah was so terrified at the conclusion of the visit that he cried: "We shall surely die, for we have seen God" (13:22). He felt God's presence and his own unworthiness, but he overstated the case if he concluded that the visitor was God in physical form. "No man has seen God" is a truth consistently affirmed in the Bible, the incarnate Son being the only exception. "He who has seen Me has seen the Father," Jesus said to Philip (John 14:9b). Throughout the Scriptures, God is portrayed as being pure spirit, protected by the second commandment against material images of any kind.

A better suggestion is that the visitor was an archangel such as Gabriel, who came to Mary with similar news of the birth of Jesus (Luke 1:19). Angels such as this one visited with Abraham, even sat down and ate with him, then traveled on to Sodom to encounter Lot (Gen. 18-19). This angelic guest, however, like the one who challenged Gideon to serve the Lord, refused to partake of food and also was awesome in his appearance and actions (6:21; 13:19-20). Christians normally do not see or become aware of the angelic protection or guidance that the Lord provides for His people. Joseph received the warning of an angel to leave Bethlehem and flee to Egypt and later the assurance of an angel that he could safely return to his own country (Matt. 2:13, 19). Both times, however, the message from God came through a dream. We also must be ever listening and prepared to heed God's guiding Word for our lives. The holy angels are indeed entrusted many times with the communication of that message.

The name given to the promised child by Manoah and his wife was Samson. It stems from the Semitic term for sun, *shemesh,* with the addition of the diminutive ending *on.* So "Little Sun," or perhaps even "Sunny-boy," was the meaning of his name. Another suggestion connects the name of Samson with the nearby village of Beth-Shemesh, just two miles away from Zorah, where he was born.

3. *The mighty champion (14:1-9)*

Exceptional talents, both physical and mental, came naturally to the youthful Samson and distinguished him from the other lads around him. His mighty feats of strength, however, were the direct result of the Spirit's power in his life. When he was old enough to undertake his initial service as judge and leader of his people, we read: "And the Spirit of the LORD began to stir him" (13:25*a*). No one could ask for a better start in life. He enjoyed every endowment a person could hope for, including godly parents who loved and cared for him in response to God's call and blessing.

Samson was eligible to marry in his late teens, but the proper procedure was to allow his parents to select his wife or at least participate in his choice. The engagement and official arrangements had to be undertaken by the fathers of the bride and groom. Yet Samson stormed into his home one day and demanded that his parents get the daughter of a certain Philistine for his wife. The shock and dismay caused by this attitude is evident in the response of his father and mother, who pleaded with him to reconsider and marry one of the Israelite girls (14:3-4). It was common to choose a wife from the cousins or near relatives of one's own clan throughout the ancient Near East. "Uncircumcised Philistines" (14:3) was a term of utter contempt in the lips of a Hebrew, and when applied to Samson's future father-in-law, it should have given him pause to reflect on what he intended to do; but he was too self-willed to care. The young hero, at this moment, was not motivated by the highest standards of honor or respect for his heritage. Nor was he led by the Spirit of holiness, even though his marriage would result in some measure of victory over the Philistines.

Marriages with foreigners were fairly common in Israel, but the Law required that the outsider first be converted to true faith in God. Ruth, the Moabite girl, confessed as she entered into the life of Naomi's people in Bethlehem, "Your God [shall be] my God" (Ruth 1:16*b*). Warnings against intermarriage with the nations of Canaan always carried the expressed intent of not allowing a pagan spouse to turn the Israelites away from God (Deut. 7:3-4). Samson, by this marriage, revealed his weakness for the lusts of the flesh that eventually led him to disaster.

It is difficult to understand this statement in the text: "It [this marriage] was of the LORD, for He was seeking an occasion against the Philistines" (14:4*a*). How could such a union with an unconverted Philistine be, in any sense, from the Lord? The answer is complex but important for Christians to consider today. The sovereign God can turn our decisions to fulfill His ends, even when we make them in transgression of His laws of holiness. Pharaoh freely determined to enslave the Hebrew tribes in Egypt, yet the Bible states, God "hardened his heart" to do this (Exod. 10:1). Rehoboam made a bad choice when he said he would add even

SAMSON AND THE PHILISTINES
→ Attacks by Samson

heavier taxes on the northern tribes, yet we read, "It was a turn of events from the LORD, that He might establish His word" (1 Kings 12:15a). In this same manner, we may conclude that Samson's decision was a wrong one, yet it was allowed by God and ordained to accomplish an initial victory over the enemies of God's people.

Samson was not the only hero to kill a lion; David and Benaiah did the same. But only Samson could tear the great beast apart "as one tears a kid" (14:6). The same verb is used here as is found in Leviticus 1:17 for tearing the wings off a bird used in sacrifice. As a ritual opening of a festive occasion, kids were also torn apart by Arab hosts before their guests. Only a man with superhuman strength, however, could so divide the body of a lion with his bare hands. Yet Samson did not mention his feat to anyone. Months later he passed that way again and discovered that the skeleton of the lion housed a swarm of bees, so he took honey from the carcass and ate it as he walked on. Honey was a supreme delight to the ancients since their world knew nothing of refined sugars or candies.

4. *Samson's wedding (14:10—15:7)*

When we read that Samson returned to the woman of Timnah with his father to make "a feast there," we may assume that this was the wedding itself (14:10). It lasted seven days, following the custom throughout the Middle East. The literal meaning of *feast* is "drinking party," certainly the wrong environment for a Nazirite who was committed to the refusal of all intoxicating drinks. Normally the bridegroom brought his own companions with him, but Samson had only his father. Could it be that his Israelite friends refused to get involved in such a marriage with one of their enemies across the border? Thirty men of the Philistines is a large group of friends of the bridegroom (14:11). This shows either the large size of the wedding feast or the Philistines' determination to be prepared for whatever Samson might try to do against them.

The riddle was a popular game in ancient Israel. When the queen of Sheba arrived to meet Solomon, she tested him with difficult questions, or riddles (1 Kings 10:1). Here the cleverness of Samson was too much for his new friends, so they put pressure on the bride to get the answer for them. During the entire week of feasting the game continued, getting more tense and bitter as the end of the feast came near. Finally, on the seventh day, the bride's tears cajoled Samson into revealing the secret of the riddle. Both problem and answer are beautiful examples of Hebrew poetry and parallelism:

> Out of the eater came something to eat,
>   And out of the strong came something sweet (14:14).
> What is sweeter than honey?
>   And what is stronger than a lion? (14:18*a*).

Samson was infuriated when the Philistines triumphantly announced the answer and won the game of the riddle on the very last minute of the seventh day. He accused them of forcing the answer out of his bride, using a rather coarse metaphor: "If you had not plowed with my heifer, you would not have found out my riddle" (14:18*b*). Samson did not charge them with an adulterous act but rather with an abuse of the confidence that should have been respected between a man and his bride.

To keep his word, Samson had to furnish thirty linen garments (undergarments) and thirty festive robes. This he did by raiding Ashkelon, one of the five major cities of the Philistines. When the Spirit of the Lord again came upon him in power, Samson fought and killed thirty men of the city, then delivered their robes to the men who won, albeit unfairly, the game of the riddle. "His anger burned" (14:19) is a close translation for the literal Hebrew expression, "with nostrils heated." Samson was too frustrated and enraged to return to his wife; he went straight to the home of his parents.

Some time must have passed, during which the father of the bride decided that Samson would never return, so he gave his daughter to a friend of Samson's, the best man of the wedding (15:2). The news of his bride's remarriage never reached Samson's ears. So, later on, when he went to visit his wife, taking with him the makings of a feast, his father-in-law refused him entrance into the house, saying, "I gave her to another man, here take her sister!" (author's translation). His offer may have been intended to satisfy Samson, but it was another bitter moment for him. Yet he blamed the treachery even more on the other Philistines who attended the wedding, and so he resolved to even the score.

Samson's revenge, burning up the grainfields of the Philistines, would have been considered among the most heinous of crimes known to the Canaanites. The god of Philistia was Dagon, the grain-god, and their livelihood as well as their food for the entire year depended upon a full harvest of grain. The Hebrew word for "foxes" may also be translated as "jackals," or "wild dogs." Jackals would have been easier to catch, since they ran in packs. A torch tied between two jackals would have moved slowly through the fields, starting fires in many places. Years later, David's son Absalom pulled a similar trick on Joab, burning up Joab's fields to get the attention he wanted (2 Sam. 14:30). It is not surprising that olive trees also were consumed; frequently the olive orchards served a double purpose, giving shade for planting smaller crops around them as well as providing their own fruit. Even the vineyards nearby were burned up, a total disaster for the farming communities of the Philistines (15:5).

The Philistines reacted by turning against their own neighbor and fellow countryman, the father of Samson's bride at Timnah. He, his family, and all his possessions were destroyed by fire to the consternation of Samson, who thereupon determined to take full revenge on these wicked enemies of his (15:6-7).

5. *Samson's victories (15:8-20)*

Samson's great slaughter may have been carried out in a series of individual battles. The description of "hip and thigh" is best understood as a position for hand-to-hand combat or a term for the ancient form of wrestling. Literally, it referred to the calf and upper leg parts of the body. Another suggestion is that in the heat of his anger, he broke the Philistines' leg bones as he vanquished them in battle. Afterward the exhausted hero escaped to a hiding place, a "cleft of the rock" of Etam, which remains unmarked, someplace in the rugged hills west of Hebron (15:8).

The story of these attacks and counterattacks comes to a climax at the place known as the "Jawbone," Lehi, mentioned also in 2 Samuel 23:11 in connection with a battle against the Philistines. This time a large armed force marched up into the foothills of Judah and demanded Samson's capture. This invasion so alarmed the people that three thousand men of Judah were immediately dispatched to find Samson. "Do you not know that the Philistines are rulers over us?" they asked him (15:11). It was a desperate state of affairs and one that Samson could not refute; it was his welfare or theirs, so he let himself be bound. All his exploits had not diminished the oppressive power of his enemies over the people of Judah.

Victory returned to Samson again, at this same place called "The Jawbone," Lehi (15:14). When the hero felt the power of the Spirit, he broke the cords that held him prisoner and fought against the Philistines, using only the fresh (more supple) jawbone of an ass. A thousand of the enemy were killed in this fight at Ramath-Lehi, "the Heights of Lehi" (15:15-17).

As a sequel to this victory, Samson experienced the providence of God in a miraculous way. In answer to his prayer that the Lord satisfy his acute thirst, a spring of water came from the "hollow place" at Lehi (15:18-19). Samson not only acknowleged himself to be God's servant (15:18), but he received that special grace that comes to the servants of God when they pray. So, by God's mercy, his life was spared and his strength returned. The spring became known as the "Spring of the Partridge," *En-hakkore,* but its name also can mean the "Spring of the one who called [on the LORD]."[2]

6. *Samson and Delilah (16:1-14)*

Samson's fatal flaw might be described as his lust for the Philistine women. Before Delilah, it was the harlot of Gaza (16:1) who attracted his attention. Perhaps he intended to visit her by slipping into the city unobserved, but his enemies

2. John Gray, *Joshua, Judges, and Ruth* (Greenwood, S.C.: Attic, 1967), p. 355.

learned of his presence and plotted to seize him. Since the gates would lock everyone in during the night, their plan was to kill him that next morning. But Samson escaped the hard way, by pulling up the gate with its posts and carrying them off to a hill in the direction of Hebron! This prodigious feat of strength must have amazed his enemies and friends alike. A double gate built with massive timbers, together with its posts and iron hinges, would have weighed many hundreds of pounds.

The third woman of the Philistines that we know about in Samson's life was Delilah from the Valley of the Sorek River, which was near his parent's home. Because the name is Semitic, many commentators assume that she was actually an Israelite who had gone over to live among the Philistines. If the name is taken from the Aramaic term *dallatum*, it meant "flirtatious," which gives added reason to suspect that she was useful for the purpose of seduction.[3] Only in this third affair do we read that Samson "loved a woman"; he was completely infatuated with her. Had she become his wife, the text would probably have mentioned that fact. It was another case of misplaced affection that again would lead to deep trouble for the Israelite judge.

Delilah, like Judas Iscariot, betrayed a friend for money. There were five lords of the Philistines, representing the five major cities of Philistia. If each one offered her eleven hundred silver shekels, the bribe would be a huge sum indeed. Gideon tallied only seventeen hundred shekels from the spoils confiscated from the Midianites (8:26), and the Levite priest received only ten shekels per year for his services to Micah in the following chapter (17:10). It is interesting to note, how-

3. C. F. Burney, *The Book of Judges* (New York: Ktav, 1970), p. 407.

ever, that the sum stolen from Micah's mother was exactly the same as this one offered to Delilah by each of the Philistine kings, eleven hundred silver shekels (17:2). An alternate translation by Robert G. Boling reads, "from each unit (elef), one hundred shekels."[4]

If Samson sensed the danger he was in, he never showed it but instead acted with typical carelessness for his personal safety. Living dangerously had been his way of life up to that point; probably he believed he could always presume on the favor and strength of the Lord. It is almost as though Samson wanted to play with fire, so to speak, and enjoy the heady feeling of winning against all odds.

7. *Samson's betrayal (16:15-31)*

Years before at Timnah, during the wedding feast, Samson's bride had used tears to obtain his secret of the riddle about the lion and the honey (14:16). Now he would be defeated again by a woman's tears and constant nagging. To Delilah's repeated questions about the source of his power, Samson at first gave playful and illusory answers. Each time the Philistines took him at his word, they were frustrated in their attempts to capture him. First they tried to hold him with new gut, then with freshly woven cords, and finally with his own locks of hair caught in a loom; but he broke away every time.

"His soul was annoyed to death" (16:16b) fittingly describes Samson's agony of soul, torn between his duty to keep his vows to the Lord and his passion for Delilah. Her tears proved stronger than his trust in God, and he told her of his Nazirite vows and the meaning of his long hair (16:17). The

4. Boling, p. 248.

next time he fell asleep, she cut his long hair before he was bound up. Still presuming on his youthful endowment, Samson awoke but "did not know that the LORD had departed from him" (16:20*b*). Believers should take heed to Samson's example and realize that it is possible to backslide in the Christian life in this same fashion. We may presume to walk in the Spirit's power when, in fact, we have forfeited His strength by our disobedience or lack of yielding to God's will. Our Lord's parents left Him in Jerusalem when He was twelve, then traveled a whole day's journey without realizing He was not with them. So we, too, may move out on our own strength and fail to realize that we have left the Holy Spirit behind.

Immediately the Philistines "gouged out his eyes" (16:21) to humiliate Samson. The blinding of prisoners of war, particularly of high officials, was fairly common in the ancient world (cf. 2 Kings 25:7). But it was even more degrading for Samson to be chained to a mill like an animal and forced to turn the axle day in and day out for the following year. However, it must have been a time for deep reflection on Samson's part, and evidently he repented of his transgressions and lack of faithfulness before God. His hair also grew out during that year in the prison and his former strength returned with it.

Meanwhile, the five rulers of Philistia had prepared a great celebration to honor their god, Dagon, and to mark the defeat of their enemy Samson. Evidently the place was Gaza, because it was both the site of the temple of Dagon and the prison where Samson had been kept. A similar temple was uncovered farther north at Tel Qasile, also belonging to the Philistines and dating to the eleventh century B.C. For the first time, a temple displayed two central pillars that upheld the roof. Located near the altar, the stone pillar bases were approximately two meters apart; their heavy wooden posts once supported the ceiling and roof of the temple. A large man could touch them with outstretched hands and, with sufficient strength, topple the entire structure.[5]

Their taunt, "Call for Samson, that he may amuse us" (16:25*a*), means literally, "Call him that he may make us laugh." The blinded ex-hero was supposed to humor them with his tortured body or by outbursts of bitter anger and frustration. Three thousand guests stared at Samson in his agony and gloated over his weakness. But a prayer went up to the true God from Samson's lips, "Strengthen me just this time, O God, that I may at once be avenged of the Philistines for my two eyes" (16:28*b*). And God replied by restoring his superhuman strength for one last great victory over the Philistines.

Samson, the judge, paid with his own life for his greatest victory over the enemies of Israel. A small step had been taken toward the liberation of the tribes, but it would be King David, a century later, who finally ended the oppressive domination of the Philistines over Israel. Samson never finished the task. He had a wonderful start in life, but too often he allowed his willfulness and fleshly desires to interfere with the call of God.

---

5. Ami Mazar, "A Philistine Temple at Tel Qasile," *The Biblical Archaeologist* 36 (1973):43. Mazar reports about a temple from the Iron Age with two pillars near the altar, about two meters apart, that supported the roof of the temple. Tel Qasile is in the northern suburbs of modern Tel Aviv.

9

FALSE WORSHIP

III. THE TRIBAL PROBLEMS OF THE JUDGES (17:1—21:25)

A. THE EPHRAIMITE, THE LEVITE, AND THE DANITES (17:1—18:31)

1. *A materialistic mother and son (17:1-5)*

TWO FINAL NARRATIVES remain to be told to give the full picture of what it meant to live in a day of moral and political disorder among the tribes and before there was a king in Israel (17:6; 18:1). Micah and his mother are sharply distinguished from Samson and his mother by their materialism and idolatry. Here there is no evidence of the presence or call of the Spirit in their lives. Rather, the point is made that the true faith had degenerated to a low level, particularly in the tribes of Dan and Benjamin. Micah, however, lived in the hill country of Ephraim.

It is convenient to place these stories, often thought of as appendices to the main account, at an earlier date when the judges were just beginning their rule over the tribes. Evidence for this may be seen in the reference to Jonathan, Moses' grandson (18:30; 20:28). The two stories are not connected to each other or to the rest of the narratives of the judges.

Micah's name, "Who is there like the Lord?" would presume a faithful mother and father who worshiped the true God according to the Mosaic revelation. Yet, he stole a huge sum of money from his mother, eleven hundred shekels, only to return it again without any explanation. The mother immediately hired a smith to form an idol of metal valued at two hundred shekels, a small part of the total sum that had been dedicated to the Lord. Micah then set up a shrine in his home for the image and added an ephod and teraphim. The ephod was probably a bejeweled priestly garment (cf. Gideon's ephod in 8:27), and the teraphim were effigies of Syrian deities. For lack of a real priest, Micah made one of his sons serve as head of his shrine (17:5). In all of this, the holy names of *Elohim* and *Yahweh* were revered, but under idolatrous forms and rites.

2. *A mercenary Levite (17:6-13)*

The shrine had a visitor, a young man from Bethlehem, who later is identified as none other than the grandson of Moses! ("Manasseh" recorded in 18:30 of the King James Version resulted from a late insertion of the letter *nun* in the original name of *Moses*.)[1] His name was Jonathan, son of Gershom, son of Moses (18:30), and he was both a Levite and a Judean. This intermingling of the tribes at such an early date is significant for understanding how the one tribe of Judah could eventually lay claim to the larger name of Israel. Paul, for example, was a Jew, that is, a Judean, but he also was of the tribe of Benjamin. It is natural to suppose that this particular Levite was well known for his famous grandfather and therefore recognized by the Danites as a person of value to them. It is harder to explain why Jonathan was wandering alone, away from his family, and why he was willing to attach himself to Micah for ten shekels of silver per year in

1. A curious and clumsily written letter *nun* was inserted in this name by some copyist, slightly above the line, to make the name "Moses" read "Manasseh."

exchange for his priestly services. For Micah, the acquisition
of a bona fide priest of the tribe of Levi was a good omen.
"Now I know that [Yahweh] will prosper me" he exclaimed
(17:13).

3. *The Danite migration (18:1-13)*

The third element in the story is the visit of a band of
Danites on their way to the far north in search of a new homeland for the tribe of Dan (18:1-2). After their initial surprise at finding the young grandson of Moses serving Micah
as a priest, the Danites demanded his professional advice for
their journey and mission. To "inquire of God" (18:5)
ought to mean seeking by prayer to know the will of God.
However, within a paganized society, it more likely involved
the use of some medium or sorcery. As usual in such situa-
tions, the answer was a positive, "Go in peace; your way . . .
has the LORD's approval" (18:6).

When the spies of Dan reached Laish, which is located at
the northern edge of the Huleh Valley, they found a quiet
city that was without fortifications and isolated from the
coastal metropolis of Sidon. Some would read the next
phrase: "no dealings with Syria" (18:7), assuming the Hebrew word *'adam,* man, was originally *'aram,* which refers to
Syria. Thus, the people of Laish were cut off from outside
interference or support from both east and west. This fea-
ture, plus the rich and fertile land around Laish, gave the
Danites ample reason to want to capture it and make it their
permanent dwelling place.

The failure of Dan to take and hold its allotted land was
one of the greatest disappointments of the Israelites in their
entire conquest of Canaan. Dan had been next to the largest
in number of all the tribes—62,700 fighting men, second

only to Judah (Num. 1:39). Not only was their retreat to the north a moral blow to the pride of Israel, but it also created a military weakness by allowing the Philistines to control the central coastline. With this loss also went the valuable port city of Joppa, which would have provided the inland tribes with trade and rich commercial opportunities. Dan should have expanded and enlarged its territory, but instead the tribe became more and more cramped as the Philistines managed to overpower them and drive them back into the foothills of Judah and Ephraim (cf. Josh. 19:47 and Judg. 1:34, where "Amorites" stand as a general designation for the local Philistines).

"When you enter, you shall come to a . . . spacious land . . . a place where there is no lack of anything that is on the earth" (18:10). Travelers who have visited the Huleh Valley and the vicinity of Dan expound on the natural resources and fertility of the area. Water comes from every rock and hill, pouring down from the nearby mountains of Lebanon. Like Scotland, this part of Galilee is green and overgrown with all forms of vegetation. The tribe of Dan had seized upon a veritable paradise on earth!

Two plots have been skillfully woven together in these chapters: the foolish behavior of Micah and the retreat to the north by the tribe of Dan. The spies, having returned with their report on Laish, informed their colleagues of the presence of a Levite-priest in Micah's household. Jonathan was evidently alone in the house when they greeted him with the traditional "Shalom" (18:15). Gentiles need to be reminded that the Hebrew term *shalom* means "wholeness," or "health," mental as well as physical. It can even imply prosperity and one's general welfare. "Peace," therefore, is a secondary meaning of *shalom*.

4. *The youthful priest (18:14-26)*

The pagan symbols used in worship were seized by the Danites. For true followers of the Law revealed through Moses, as well as for Christians today, such interest in heathen idols is an abomination. But the narration of this and similar failures of the tribes during those days was precisely the intention of the prophetic mind and the Spirit who composed the book of Judges. Such was the bad state of affairs when "every man did what was right in his own eyes" (17:6*b*).

"Be to us a father and a priest" (18:19) echoed the full title given to the young Levite by Micah when he was first hired as the household priest (17:10). This figurative use of "father" can be traced far back into patriarchal times. Joseph, for example, became "a father to Pharaoh" (Gen. 45:8). Frequently it carried the meaning of a spiritual father, as when the younger Elisha cried out at Elijah's departure, "My father, my father" (2 Kings 2:12). But Jesus instructed His disciples: "You are all brothers. . . . Do not call anyone on earth your father" (Matt. 23:8-9). We who are still the disciples of one Master and Lord should employ such honorific titles with great caution.

There is an amusing scene following the capture of the priest and his ritual paraphernalia. Micah gathered a company of his neighbors together and ran after the Danite troop to demand their return. "What is the matter with you?" the Danites shouted at him (18:23*b*). "You have taken away my gods which I made . . . and what do I have besides?" Micah shouted right back (18:24*a*). Poor Micah's cries were wasted on the Danites, who threatened his life if he persisted in shouting at them. They continued on their way, putting their "little ones and the livestock and the valuables in front of them" (18:21*b*). Read "their valuables" in verse 21 rather than "their carriage," as the King James Version translates it.

So Micah faded from the scene, being too weak to defend his holy objects or his hired priest. We may remember Micah as a frustrated and misguided Israelite who turned from the faith of his fathers and justly suffered the consequences of his own sins.

5. *The fall of Laish (18:27-31)*

The seizure of Laish follows the patterns of conquest under Joshua, when he took cities such as Jericho and Hazor; the holy "ban" consigned all the inhabitants to destruction, and Laish itself was burned to the ground. It was renamed after Dan, the son of Jacob, father of the tribe of Dan. Jonathan, the priest taken from the household of Micah, became the father of a long dynasty of Levitical priests in the city of Dan. "Until the day of capitvity of the land" (18:30) cannot mean until the invasion by the Assyrians in 734 B.C., as some suggest, since this date would be too late for the historical nature of the writing of the book of Judges. It more likely means the coming of the monarchy under David and Solomon during the tenth century, when these northern tribal areas were brought under centralized rule. However, it could also be a reference to an early captivity under the Syrians (1 Sam. 14:47) or one under the Philistines at the time they overran the country and ruined the holy place at Shiloh (1 Sam. 4:11, 22). This last suggestion fits into the next statement (18:31) on the duration of the graven image.

10

LAWLESS LUST

B. THE LEVITE'S CONCUBINE (19:1-30)

THE PREVIOUS NARRATIVE illustrated the shame of false worship among the tribes in those days "when there was no king in Israel" (19:1). This final story will reveal the violence and immorality that prevailed. From the tribes of Ephraim and Dan, we turn to the Benjaminites, but again a Levite played the leading role and the city of Bethlehem was involved.

In ancient Israel, a concubine was usually a wife of low estate, with only part of the status rightfully belonging to a full marriage covenant. This Levite was a man of some means, having a servant and animals as well as a concubine. His residence was in the northern hills of Ephraim, but his concubine was a native of Bethlehem in Judah.

1. *A family quarrel (19:1-21)*

"And his concubine became angry with him" (19:2) is a more probable translation for this obscure passage than the King James Version, which reads, "And his concubine played the whore against him." Had she committed adultery, in all likelihood he would have sought her death or refused to take her back into his home. Instead, he traveled to the city of

Bethlehem to "speak tenderly to her" and persuade her to return with him. Evidently he was at fault, not she.

A three-day visit would have been normal, but the father-in-law kept his guest two extra days with feasting, drinking, and festivities, apparently seeking to secure his goodwill and the kind treatment of his daughter in the future.

A trip from Bethlehem to the western edge of Jerusalem would have taken two or three hours, and by the time they arrived at this point, the afternoon was ending. Yet Jerusalem was not considered a proper place to pass the night, since it belonged to "foreigners," an observation that is ironic in the story since it was not strangers but children of Israel who assaulted the concubine and degraded the entire nation. Jebus had been the local name for the "City of the Jebusites," which the tribe of Benjamin should have conquered because it was placed within Benjamin's land allotment by Joshua (Josh. 18:16). It would be left to David and his men to capture the city of Jerusalem and make it Israel's capital.

The sun was going down when the small party reached Gibeah, four miles directly north of Jerusalem (19:14). William Albright excavated this site, known by the Arabs as Tell el-Ful; he found indications of a fortress with double walls and four corner towers from the time of Saul's reign in the eleventh century. Previously there could have been a small Canaanite settlement, but little evidence is extant for the city of Gibeah as described in this passage.[1] The weary travelers were met with inhospitality by the local Benjaminites until another Ephraimite, who was residing there, saw them and offered his house for the night's lodging (19:15-

1. William F. Albright, *The Archaeology of Palestine,* rev. ed. (Harmondsworth, Eng.: Penguin, 1960), pp. 120-21.

21). Already the Benjaminites had shown their base and degenerated state, since kindness to strangers has always been
a common virtue in the East. But in the house of the old man
from Ephraim, the travelers found comfort and food.

2. *A lesson in terror (19:22-30)*

The outrage that followed bore close resemblance to the
account of the two angels who visited Lot's house in Sodom
(Gen. 19). Like the angels, this guest was a man of special
merit, in this case a Levite. He had identified his destination
as the "house of the Lord" (19:18, KJV), which meant the
holy place at Shiloh, farther to the north in Ephraim. Like
the Sodomites, the wicked men of Gibeah demanded the use
of the visitor for sexual abuses; they, too, were labeled "worth-
less fellows" (19:22). Belial in this text in the King James
Version should not be capitalized or thought of as the devil
or some evil spirit, because the personification of the term did
not come into use until during and after the intertestamental
period (cf. 2 Cor. 6:15). As in the case of Lot, this host offered his own daughter and the concubine to the angry crowd
outside as a means of sparing his honored guest the shame
and abuse that the men of the town intended.

Some defect in the culture of those days needs to be recognized, for certainly the women were treated as more "expend-
able" than the men. Nor can we excuse the lack of chivalry
simply because the women in this case were younger or of a
low caste. The enormity of the crime and the depravity of
the men of Gibeah can hardly be exaggerated. Many years
later the prophet Hosea mentioned this act as a historic example of evil (Hos. 9:9; 10:9). We can only condemn the
Levite for a selfish and inhuman deed when he thrust out his

own wife for the obvious brutalization he knew was coming.

In the morning her dead body was at the doorstep of the house, hands outstretched toward the threshold in a final appeal for help. Christians in the modern world must never take lightly the evil results of sexual perversion and homosexuality; terrible acts of violence and sadism go hand in hand with these same forms of immorality within our own loose and indulgent society.

11

TRIBAL WAR

C. THE BENJAMINITE WAR (20:1-48)

ISRAEL'S REACTION to the evil deed done to the Levite's concubine in Gibeah shows that a measure of righteousness still prevailed among the tribes. The crude means of informing the tribes of what had happened—cutting the body of the concubine into twelve sections and sending them throughout the land—was nevertheless effective. Scholars have tried to deny the presence of twelve tribes during the early period of the judges; here is strong confirmation of their existence. Twelve was the exact number of the tribal land portions; counting the Levites, the tribes actually numbered thirteen.

1. *Preparations for battle (20:1-17)*

Chapter 20 opens with the assembly of outraged Israelites gathered at Mizpah (spelled Mizpeh in the King James Version), only a few miles north of Gibeah and right on the border of Benjamin (20:1). The moment was grave, with the horrors of a civil war hanging in the balance, so the men carefully reviewed the evidence for the crime committed by certain men at Gibeah against the Levite and his concubine. The guilty ones were named and sent for, but the Benjaminites refused to extradite them to be executed. Thus the war against Benjamin was inevitable (20:12-14).

Four hundred thousand Israelites fighting against 26,700 Benjaminites seems like overwhelming odds, yet the initial victories went to the smaller force of Benjaminites. Recognition is given to the superior skills of the stone-slingers of Benjamin (20:16). Four hundred thousand men of the tribes, however, is a difficult number to fit into the historical situation of Palestine at the time of the judges, even though it corresponds to the number of men who came out of Egypt under Moses when you make allowance for sizable losses or the noncooperation of certain tribes. Perhaps here again the term translated "thousand," *elef,* may actually represent a military contingent provided by a single clan, normally ten fighting men but at times as many as thirty. Calculated on this basis, the actual numbers participating in this war would have been much smaller than most translations indicate.

This theory will not work, however, in the case of Benjamin, whose army of 26,000 would then be only 780 men to start with (26 *elefs* times 30). Nor does it harmonize with the mathematical data presented in 20:9-11, where *elef* clearly means one thousand men. From every standpoint, the battle statistics are a puzzle.

Bethel appears in the story as a place to inquire of the Lord (20:18), which makes this one of the earliest records of a shrine there. In patriarchal times an altar had been erected at Bethel by Abraham (Gen. 12:8; 13:3) and another by Jacob upon his return from the land of Haran (Gen. 35:1). But at the time of this crisis between the tribes, it seems that even the Ark of the Covenant had been moved to Bethel from its usual place in Shiloh. Phinehas, the grandson of Aaron and son of the high priest, Eleazar (20:28), was placed in charge of the holy place at Bethel. The first thing this indicates is the timing of the war with Benjamin within the initial days of the judges and shortly after the death of Joshua, since the grandchild of Aaron was still living. The second thing that becomes clear is the confusion of places to worship. Moses had commanded that there be one place for the name of the Lord to dwell in (Deut. 12:5, 11, 14). Already this Mosaic order was being transgressed by the tribes. A shrine at Gilgal continued to be frequented by the Israelites in those days, and to make matters worse, the Danites had set up their own worship center at Laish-Dan in the north.

2. *Wins and losses (20:18-48)*

The question "Who shall go up first for us to battle against the sons of Benjamin?" (20:18*a*) means, "Which tribe should lead the others and bear the full onslaught of the battle?" God answered them, but for two successive days the battles went against the greater armies of Israel and in favor of the men of Benjamin. So again the people went to the shrine to inquire of the Lord, this time weeping in dismay for their defeats (20:26; notice that the weeping is mentioned twice, vv. 23 and 26, and could be understood as happening on two occasions, once at the end of each day of defeat).

Then an entire day was set aside for fasting, burnt offerings, peace offerings, and prayer also, as indicated by their attempts to inquire for the will of God. The priest gave them a message of reassurance. The Lord promised, "tomorrow I will deliver them into your hand" (20:28*b*). The people responded with the total dedication of their lives, as indicated by the burnt offerings and their thankfulness and trust, which was symbolized in their peace offerings.

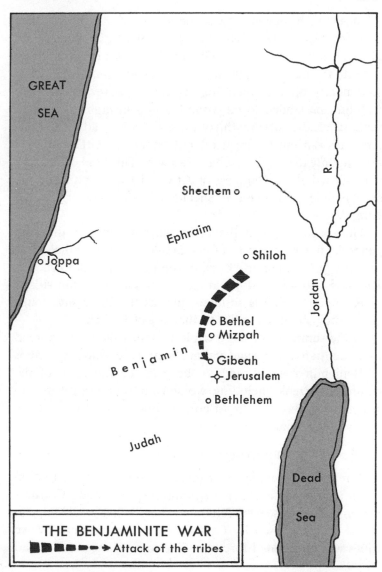

THE BENJAMINITE WAR
▰▰▰▰▰▰➤ Attack of the tribes

An ambush, however, was the secret of the success that followed. Literally translated, verse 29 reads, "And Israel placed waiting ones around Gibeah." It was a ruse that drew out into the open the fighting men of Benjamin, and as a result, nearly all the offending tribesmen were killed. The Israelites pretended to be wounded and in flight along two separate roads, but only thirty were actually dead. The Benjaminites ran out to finish off the Israelites as they feigned retreat, only to find themselves trapped. This kind of strategy had worked at the conquest of Ai when Joshua attacked the second time, and again at Shechem in the days of the evil King Abimelech (9:43).

The specification of places in the battle marks the area generally north and east of Gibeah and south of Bethel. The location of Baal-tamar, "Lord of the Palm," is unknown; but Rimmon (20:45) is still marked by the modern Arab village of Ramman, which is situated, just as the Bible says, on a rocky spur about five miles to the east of Bethel.

In the summary of the terrible losses of the war, we read that twenty-five thousand valiant men were killed, the cities of Benjamin were burned to the ground, and most of the common citizens, including women and children, were destroyed. Only six hundred Benjaminites were known to have survived this final battle (20:47).

D. PEACE BETWEEN THE TRIBES (21:1-25)

A remarkable change of heart and spirit of reconciliation set in almost as soon as the sounds of war ended. Consternation and remorse were felt on all sides. What would happen to the nation chosen by God if one of the original twelve tribes was obliterated forever? The internecine conflict had been even harder on the families than on the men of Benjamin. Where would the remnant of six hundred get wives for the rebuilding of the tribe? At Mizpah, in the fervor of righteous indignation, all Israel had sworn a solemn vow never again to give their daughters in marriage to the men of Benjamin (21:1).

Another vow had been taken at Mizpah before the battle, however, and this had to do with a "great oath" against any clan or tribe that failed to rally in support of the punitive war against the Benjaminites. So, when it was revealed that the people of Jabesh-gilead had refused to cooperate in the battle, a plan was contrived to "kill two birds with one stone." An army would be sent to destroy Jabesh-gilead in fulfillment of the oath, and at the same time, a company of virgins would be seized and turned over to the tribe of Benjamin. Therefore, 12,000 men were assigned to attack the Trans-Jordan city of Jabesh-gilead, where another horrible slaughter took place. All the city's inhabitants were slain except for 400 young, marriageable women. The virgins of Jabesh-gilead were brought back into "the land of Canaan" (21:12; notice the indication that Canaan, as defined in the Old Testament, did not extend east of the Jordan River).

Meanwhile, the 600 survivors of the tribe of Benjamin had been hiding out in the wilderness to the east of Gibeah and Bethel at the place called the "rock of Rimmon" (see 20:45; 21:13). Overtures of peace and the offer of wives brought them out of their hiding places, and it is natural that women of Jabesh-gilead would have a special kinship with the men from the tribe of Benjamin. Evidence of a strong sympathy between the two peoples is found in the defense of Jabesh-gilead some years later by Saul, the Benjaminite king, and in their loyalty and respect for him (1 Sam. 21:11; cf. also 1 Chron. 7:12, 17).

Did the Israelites blame the entire war on the Lord? So it might sound from a casual reading of 21:15*b*: "because the LORD had made a breach in the tribes of Israel." After-thoughts of compassion are natural in the wake of horrifying deeds of violence between brothers and families of the same nation. God had ordained that their own evil deeds bring about their self-inflicted judgment, and they had only them-selves to blame.

Two hundred men of Benjamin still needed wives, how-ever, and the vow of Mizpah prevented anyone from giving his daughter to them in marriage (21:18). A convenient way had to be found not only to preserve their honor, but also to restore the families of Benjamin. This led to the last and final drama of the book of Judges, the abduction of the dancing maidens.

At Shiloh it was customary to celebrate the annual feasts with gaiety and dancing. The feast at the time of the vintage was called a *hag,* literally, a "pilgrimage"; it represented the joy of the farmers in their harvesting of the grapes.[1] Young girls always danced in the open air next to the vineyards (21:19-21). Dancing as a religious ritual was an ancient cus-tom among the Canaanites, from whom the Israelites evi-dently adopted the practice.

Some have understood the "daughters of Shiloh" to be a company of women living at the holy place and serving there in some capacity. However, it is natural that they were girls from all parts of Israel, having arrived for the festival with

1. John Gray, *Joshua, Judges, and Ruth* (Greenwood, S.C.: Attic, 1967), p. 394.

their families. When they were seized one by one by the men of Benjamin, the losses were anticipated and evenly divided among the other tribes. The elders were prepared to answer any complaint with the story of the war and the tragedy by which all the former wives were killed (21:22).

All of this was irregular, of course, but such things were bound to happen back in those days when "there was no king in Israel; everyone did what was right in his own eyes" (21:25). This famous byword with which the book ends is usually thought of as a description of the state of anarchy. This is partly correct, of course, since there was neither prophet nor king to guide the nation. But the families and tribes remained intact, and the strong blood-ties continued as the people acted together within their local communities and under their elders. Times of apostasy they were, when the ways of the Canaanites were followed—years of enslavement and disaster. Yet, the tribes retained enough faith in the Lord God to pray in crises for mercy and deliverance. Not forgotten was the covenant of the Lord under Moses, and the tabernacle at Shiloh stood firm for many generations as a sign of God's promise to Israel. The Spirit of the Lord had not failed to work on their behalf through the heroic judges, even though the spiritual power of these men was all too often diminished by their human passions or lack of understanding of the will of God.

The times of the judges were difficult times indeed, but better days followed, and the story of Ruth is the bridge that leads to those days.

INTRODUCTION TO THE BOOK
OF RUTH

TURNING FROM THE BOOK of Judges to Ruth, we leave the scene of national wars and heroes to enjoy a quiet, pastoral tale. The story takes place in the Judean town of Bethlehem, surrounded by grainfields that gave it its name, "House of Bread." Bethlehem is first mentioned in connection with the tragic death of Rachel as she gave birth to Benjamin (Gen. 35:19; 48:7). Joshua assigned the village to the tribe of Judah after the conquest of the Canaanites. Twice we encounter Bethlehem in the book of Judges. It was the city of the Levite priest who joined the Danites and also the hometown of the Ephraimite's concubine, whose sadistic murder by the Benjaminites was the motive for the war between the tribes (Judg. 19).

Bethlehem owes its fame in the Old Testament to the fact that it was the place where David grew up and watched the flocks of his father, Jesse. Because of King David, this story of Ruth and Boaz was canonized and placed within the Holy Scriptures. Their child, Obed, became the grandfather of the great king.

An earlier designation of this area is Ephrathah, meaning "fruitful place." Both appellations are given in Ruth 1:2 and 4:11, as well as in the Genesis passages mentioned above (cf. Mic. 5:2 in the prophecy of the Messiah's birthplace). The name "Ephrathah" occurs too early to be linked to the tribe of Ephraim, as some have suggested it should be linked. It is clearly a place name and also a personal name (1 Chron. 2:19). Bethlehem was indeed a "fruitful place," for shepherds as well as farmers.

A time of drought would change all of this, causing a famine of grain to spread over the land, one of the worst afflictions known to man. But famines were not frequent; we know of one earlier in the days of Joseph and another years later when Elijah was the prophet in Israel (1 Kings 17:1). Sometimes a famine resulted from the ravages of war or military oppression. If this were the case for the famine in the story of Ruth, we might calculate that one of the nations that oppressed the tribes during the time of the judges caused this affliction. Midian, for example, stripped the land of its produce as far south as Gaza, including the area around Bethlehem. This reconstruction would make Ruth and Boaz contemporaries of Gideon during the early times of the judges.

DATE OF COMPOSITION

The events of the book should be reckoned no earlier than the twelfth century B.C., because Boaz was only four generations from King David. But a difficulty arises in the earlier lineage of Boaz, who is linked to the days of Joshua by his father, Salmon, husband of Rahab (Matt. 1:5). How could this be if the conquest took place at 1400 B.C.? Even the late date of 1250 B.C. makes it problematic for Boaz to be the son of Rahab and Salmon. We must assume either a gap in the genealogies or exceptionally long lives, making Boaz an old man when he married Ruth.

The writing of the story of Ruth is usually dated in the

tenth century B.C., during the reign of David or Solomon. The presence of the brief genealogy in the final chapter of Ruth supports this dating, as does the inclusion of an explanation for an old custom that had ceased to be practiced, the exchange of the sandal (4:7).

Liberal scholars have tried to substantiate a post-exilic writer for the book of Ruth. They say that the tale was invented to offset the ban against foreign wives placed upon the returned exiles by Ezra and Nehemiah. Thus they say that a book of fiction, Ruth, was written to show that even the great King David had a foreign ancestor in his family. But the early and traditional date still enjoys wide support among scholars and has the backing of the Jewish Talmud.[1]

GREAT THEMES

The nature of God is brought out in this little book with much greater detail than might appear from a casual reading. He is Lord of the forces of nature as well as the Ruler of all peoples and nations. The famine ended when the Lord "visited His people in giving them food" (1:6*b*). The deaths in Naomi's family and all the tragic experiences she suffered were directly attributed to the Lord (1:13, 21). On the other hand, when she heard the good news that Ruth had gleaned in the field of their close relative Boaz, she exclaimed, "May he be blessed of the LORD who has not withdrawn his kindness to the living and to the dead" (2:20*a*). A strong monotheism is evident throughout the story of Ruth—all that happened came from the hand of God.

The meaning of "redeemer" is illustrated by the care Boaz

---

1. Ronald M. Hals, *The Theology of the Book of Ruth* (Philadelphia: Fortress, 1969), pp. 65ff. These pages in this book review recent scholarly discussion about the date and composition of Ruth.

undertook for Naomi's household. He accepted the role of the *goel,* the male relative who was responsible for the protection and wellbeing of the two widows. An ancient law, the law of levirate marriage, required that a brother-in-law or other male kinsman of the deceased husband marry a widow who had no son in order to perpetuate the name of the deceased and provide for the widow. Thus, Boaz became not only Ruth's "redeemer," but he provided salvation for Naomi as well.

International marriages were not unequivocally outlawed in Israel. Moses, who married first a Midianite and then a Cushite, warned only against any marriage with an unbeliever who might "turn your heart" away from the Lord. In this delightful narrative, Ruth became a convert to the God of the Hebrews when she said, "Your God [shall be] my God" (1:16).

OUTLINE OF RUTH

I. The tragedies in Moab (1:1-18)
II. The return to Bethlehem (1:19-22)
III. The fields of Boaz (2:1-23)
IV. The marriage proposal (3:1-18)
V. The kinsman-redeemer (4:1-12)
VI. The marriage of Ruth and Boaz (4:13-17)
VII. The genealogy of David (4:18-22)

1

PERSONAL TRAGEDIES

I. THE TRAGEDIES IN MOAB (1:1-18)

"IN THE DAYS when the judges governed" (1:1*a*) takes us back from the writer's time into 1100 B.C., long before Samuel and the kings united the tribes into a single monarchy. Whatever animosity toward the Moabites that may have lingered after the assassination of the Moabite king by Ehud (Judg. 3:15-30) was not sufficient to prevent a family of Judah from migrating and settling down in the "land of Moab" (1:1). This area was probably the high, fertile plateau to the south of the Arnon River, a plateau that enjoys rains from clouds that pass over the Judean desert, dropping water on the higher hills of Moab. The "Ephrathites," as they were called from the name of the region around Bethlehem, also found themselves in a culture with similar language and customs.

Hebrew names usually carry a message that at times seems to be prophetic of the destiny of the characters involved. The father's name, Elimelech, "to whom God is king," was a testimony to his religious faith. His wife, Naomi, was "the pleasant one," and his two sons, Mahlon and Chilion, were, respectively, "the weakling" and "the pining one." Orpah and Ruth are foreign names and have no clear Hebrew meanings, although Ruth bears some resemblances to the word for "friend."

The life of sojourners, or migrants, in a foreign land (1:1) was never easy, since they could not buy or hold their own land. They would be forced to serve others for meager wages and join widows and orphans on the lowest level of the economy in Moab. Whatever the adversities, the three men of the family died during the ten years spent in Moab. To make the situation even more tragic, they all died without leaving sons or grandsons to carry on the family name and legal rights. Naomi was, in the language of the apostle Paul, "a widow indeed." She had nothing left for her daughters-in-law but to suggest that they should return to their mothers' houses (1:8).

It is a commendation of Naomi's character that the two girls wanted to remain with her and even return with her to her homeland. She thanked them, saying, "May the LORD deal kindly with you as you have dealt with the dead and with me" (1:8b). Orpah was finally persuaded to return, "but Ruth clung to her" (1:14b). Then from Ruth's lips came the most beautiful vow of friendship and loyalty to be found in all of literature. The words are tender and compassionate, a heart-stirring plea not to be sent away and a total commitment to follow the life and faith of Naomi. It ends with the formal language of a vow, sealing her decision to give the rest of her life to her mother-in-law (1:16-17).

The conversion of Ruth to the true religion may have been the most difficult part of her decision. Orpah had gone back not only to her people but also to her gods (1:15). This must have been tempting for Ruth, because paganism held a morbid fascination for the ancient world. The god of the Moabites was called Chemosh, whose worship involved wild celebrations and even the rites of human sacrifice.[2] Ruth was willing to leave all of this and follow the faith and laws of God that were established under Moses for Israel.

II. THE RETURN TO BETHLEHEM (1:19-22)

Naomi's return caused a sensation in Bethlehem; the Hebrew word translated "stirred" in 1:19 indicates a noisy commotion, a buzzing like the sound of bees. The rumors of her losses were confirmed immediately by Naomi. Bereaved of husband and sons, she was the object of pity. Tongues wagged with news of the foreign girl who had accompanied her from Moab, but Ruth soon earned the respect of the townspeople.

"Do not call me ['Pleasant One']; call me [the 'Troubled One,'] for the Almighty has dealt very bitterly with me," exclaimed Naomi (1:20). *Mara* has the literal meaning of a bitter taste, but in its figurative sense it need not express bitterness of spirit, but simply sadness and grief. Naomi wanted to say that her life had been one of heartache since leaving her fellow townsmen ten years before. She was now "empty" and destitute.

God is addressed as *Shadday,* "the Mighty One," a divine name found frequently in Genesis and Job in combination with the form *El,* the combined name meaning "God Almighty" (Gen. 43:14). Some link it to an old Akkadian word for "rock" or "mountain," others to a cognate term in Arabic for "strength"; hence, "the Mighty One."[3] Of course the actual name for God, the name He gave Himself, was

2. William F. Albright, *Yahweh and the Gods of Canaan* (Garden City: Doubleday, 1969), pp. 239-40.
3. Edmond Jacob, *Theology of the Old Testament* (New York: Harper & Bros., 1958), p. 46. Jacob prefers to interpret the divine name *shadday* as the "Mountain One."

Yahweh (Jehovah is a mispronunciation), and Naomi did not hesitate to refer to Him by this sacred name. The Jewish custom of not repeating this most solemn of names but substituting the more general term for Lord, *Adonai,* came after the Old Testament was completed.

The time of the grain harvest in Bethlehem would have been late April or early May, and barley was usually the first of the grains to be ripe for harvesting. The Passover and Feast of Unleavened Bread could still have been in progress when the two women returned to Bethlehem, but such a joyful, festive occasion was in sharp contrast to their dejected state of mind.

2

TRUSTING GOD

III. The Fields of Boaz (2:1-23)

Boaz is introduced into the story ahead of schedule as the "kinsman" of Naomi's deceased husband. However, this is an unfortunate translation (King James Version), because the word here is not *goel,* which will be used later for "kinsman-redeemer." The actual term in 2:1 is *moda',* which means an "acquaintance" or "friend" of Elimelech. The status of Boaz in the community is reflected in his title, "man of wealth," which also means an influential landowner and member of the respected upper class. Gideon enjoyed this same title and rank (Judg. 6:12).

Ruth offered to go in search of food along with the poor, who were allowed to pick up grain left behind by the reapers. "And she happened to come to the portion of the field belonging to Boaz" (2:3b), or so it must have seemed from her perspective. Yet, God's providential hand can be traced in every detail of the story, including this encounter with Boaz; so it was not by chance but according to God's will that she was there and that he came to her aid. It is evident that Boaz was congenial to those of the lower class who sought to take a little grain for themselves. His workers had not hindered her in any way.

"My daughter," he called her (2:8), showing the differ-ence in their ages. So a permanent welcome was extended to Ruth by Boaz; she was even given the privilege of drinking the water drawn by the reapers. Her response was to bow to the ground and express her amazement that he should be so gracious to a foreigner. There is a clever play on words in her reply: "take notice" and "foreigner" (2:10) sound almost the same in Hebrew. Boaz showed the highest of motives as he voiced his admiration for Ruth's dedication to her mother-in-law. Then his generous nature immediately revealed itself as he shared bread and wine from his own meal and ordered extra grain to be set out for her.

Ruth impressed Boaz by her decision to follow the God of Israel. His previous knowledge of her faith shows in his remark, "the God of Israel, under whose wings you have come to seek refuge" (2:12b). The same word translated "wings" can also mean "skirt," and it will occur again in the next chapter when she asks him to marry her (3:9). Union of the individual believer with God is therefore expressed in the same way as union between man and wife. The hus-band took the initiative and offered his protective name and love to the one who would share his life and work in a per-manent covenant of trust. From this beautiful phrase, "under His wings," we should not picture the mother-bird image but the care of a devoted husband for his wife. God's people are challenged to love Him as Lord with all their hearts, souls, and might (Deut. 6:5). In effect, the first command-ment declared: "I am your husband; you shall have no other husbands but Me." How often the Israelites became way-ward and "adulterous" by following after idols and by trans-gressing the Law. Yet, as the message of Hosea illustrated,

the Lord's grace always led them back. "I will betroth you
to Me forever; yes, I will betroth you to Me in righteousness
and in justice, in loving-kindness and in compassion" (Hos.
2:19).

Gleaning was the work of collecting the stalks of grain,
and more often than not, it referred to the gathering of the
stalks that were left by the reapers. It was always followed
by the business of threshing. Ruth was generously allowed
to use the area set aside for threshing, as well as whatever
equipment was available. The hand tool was a heavy wooden
rod, hinged in the middle to enable the worker to pound the
stalks of grain. Immediately after the grain was loosened
from the stalks, a fork was employed to lift the grain into the
air, allowing the wind to drive off the chaff and straw while
the heavier kernels of grain fell in a pile on the ground. At
other times, the cattle were walked back and forth over the
straw to separate the kernels from the stalks. A kind of sled
also was used for this same purpose. Threshing floors needed
to be flat areas of pounded earth or smooth rock and were
always out in the open where the winds were strong. Ruth
had worked long and hard that first day, but she had collected a full *ephah* of grain, about three-fourths of a bushel.

Naomi was amazed to see so much grain from one day's
labor. Evidently the begging poor seldom received so much
under ordinary circumstances as Ruth was able to bring
home. When she discovered, however, who the landowner
was and how Ruth had been so warmly received, Naomi
broke out in praise to God: "May he be blessed of the LORD
who has not withdrawn his kindness to the living and to the
dead" (Ruth 2:20*a*). She immediately identified Boaz as
one of her husband's cousins or relatives, one of the *goelim*,

the "kinsman-redeemers" of the clan. This was good news for the two women, and from this point their fortunes began to change. Ruth continued to glean in the fields of Boaz throughout the entire season. "All my harvest" (2:21) refers to the wheat ingathering that came about a month later than the harvest of the barley. The steady, faithful labors of Ruth on behalf of her mother-in-law continued throughout the entire period of the harvest. Normally this was the time between the Feast of the Unleavened Bread and the Feast of Pentecost, the seven weeks for the reaping of the grain. It was all gathered and harvested by the early part of June (cf. Exod. 23:16; 34:22; Num. 28:26).

IV. THE MARRIAGE PROPOSAL (3:1-18)

"Shall I not seek security for you?" was Naomi's way of saying, "Is it not my duty to find you a husband?" (3:1). The original word for *security* means a "home"—a place of rest and safety that could only be found in the protective care of a husband in that culture. Would Boaz ever consider asking Ruth to be his wife? It must have been clear that Naomi herself was out of the question. But he had shown unusual kindness and admiration for Ruth in spite of her being so much younger than he. Had Boaz been a brother of Elimelech, the law of levirate marriage would have obliged him to marry Naomi. But since he was a more distant kinsman, there existed only a moral obligation that he held in common with the other male members of the family. This law of the "brothers," as the term *levirate* indicates, is illustrated in the family trials of Judah (Gen. 38) and in the Mosaic legislation (Deut. 25:5-10). It was widely practiced throughout the entire world of the ancient Near East. Even the first-century Jews understood its meaning, as the question of the Sadducees to Jesus in Matthew 22:23-27 shows.

Ruth's way of offering herself in marriage to Boaz, following the coaching of her mother-in-law, may seem extremely unconventional to Western eyes. Having washed and prepared herself as a bride in her finest clothes, she went out to find him in the cover of night, when she knew he would be asleep. The landowner always stayed out with his men in the open air near the piles of grain to guard them from being robbed. Ruth "uncovered his feet" (3:7) and lay down quietly beside him. The Hebrew word for *feet* may also refer to his limbs. It was a courageous thing to do, but Ruth followed Naomi's instructions to the last detail.

About midnight Boaz was startled from his sleep and bent over to discover that a woman was there beside him. His shock and surprise are registered in the question, "Who are you?" (3:9a). Ruth had to be direct and open with her plea that he take her as his wife. In effect her words could be paraphrased to say, "I am your servant girl; I ask you to marry me, and I remind you that you are my redeemer" (3:9). Literally she said, "I ask you to spread your skirt over me." To this unexpected proposal, Boaz responded with pleasure and praise for her actions. There is no hint that she had done something improper to cause him embarrassment. He was amazed that she sought marriage with a man of his age. Why would she do it unless she were first of all concerned for the total welfare of her mother-in-law and the name of her family? Everything about Ruth had impressed him favorably, and he paid her one of the highest compliments possible when he said that all the townspeople esteemed Ruth to be a "woman of virtue." This is the identical term used for Boaz himself in 2:1 that is usually translated "man of wealth." It covered the qualities of good reputation and class respectability. So, Ruth the poor foreign girl had in such a brief period earned this high title of honor.

There was still one legal problem to be solved before a marriage could take place between Ruth and Boaz. Another "kinsman-redeemer" had a claim to the estate of Elimelech before Boaz. If he should want to redeem it, he had the priority and would have to be informed of the situation. Boaz promised to confront him the next day; whatever the outcome, Ruth was to fear no more, for she had his vow to see that she and Naomi would be cared for (3:13).

Ruth slipped away while it was still dark in order to return home undetected. No intimacy could have taken place between them during that night, if for no other reason than the need to respect the rights of the other kinsman-redeemer who might yet decide to mary her. However, Boaz made her take a generous amount of grain as a gift to Naomi and as a symbol of his consideration for her. Perhaps this gift was a kind of "earnest" in anticipation of all the many good things he intended to share with her in the future. After Ruth arrived home and recounted the details of her night with Boaz, it was this gift of grain that convinced Naomi that he fully intended to carry out his promise.

3

REWARD OF FAITH

V. THE KINSMAN-REDEEMER (4:1-12)

SO MUCH OF IMPORTANCE happened at the city gate in ancient Israel. It was the meetingplace for the townsmen and the outsiders who came in for the marketing and business of the day. It was the high court of the elders, who were frequently called upon to settle quarrels between the citizens. It was also the public forum, where legal transactions before witnesses were carried on. Elimelech owned a small portion of land that he had leased to someone outside the family, evidently to meet the family's needs during the famine. Naomi could not sell it in the normal sense of the word, because private property stayed within the families, or at least had to be returned to the original family. That is, it had to be "redeemed" by some legal representative of the clan. Boaz challenged the other kinsman to meet this obligation and buy up the portion. He also called together ten elders as witnesses to the affair.

The property in question must have had some significance or commercial value, because the other relative immediately showed his interest in becoming the responsible owner (4:4). One of them had to buy it "on behalf of Naomi," and up to this point the other kinsman was agreeable. Then Boaz reminded him that he would also have to buy it "on behalf of Ruth," since her dead husband, Mahlon, had been the rightful heir. This was more complicated; it required that Ruth become the wife of the kinsman and that her first son be named the new heir of the portion of land. This was too much trouble; it would have meant a division of lands and inheritance to the detriment of the kinsman's own family and sons. "Redeem it for yourself; . . . for I cannot redeem it," he replied as the ten witnesses looked on (4:6*b*).

From the expression "in former times" (4:7), we may conclude that the author of Ruth belonged to a later period, when such archaic customs were no longer practiced or understood. There was, however, a law of the sandal in the Mosaic legislation. Deuteronomy 25:5-10 covered a slightly different situation involving the right of the widow to be "redeemed" by one of the brothers-in-law. If he refused to do it, then she was allowed to shame him publicly by removing his sandal and spitting in his face! In the book of Ruth, the willing transfer of the shoe from one man to another symbolized merely the finality of the covenant agreement between them. Upon this renouncement by the other kinsman, Boaz became the legal "redeemer" (*goel*). At last he was free to marry Ruth and take over the obligations for the land that belonged to Naomi's husband and sons.

There was a second benefit gained by the action of Boaz. Now the name of Elimelech, Chilion, and Mahlon would not be forgotten, or "cut off from his brothers," as feared (4:10). Certainly this restoration of name and reputation is one of the most beautiful and significant aspects of the role of the "redeemer." As this concept passed over into the theological language of the Bible, we find the prophet Isaiah

exclaiming: "Do not fear, for I have redeemed you; I have
called you by name; you are Mine" (Isa. 43:1*b*). The individual is never forgotten or lost in the sight or to the mind of
God; thus with hope Job could cry out in his affliction, "I
know that my Redeemer lives" (Job 19:25*a*).

The Lord promised Moses that He would redeem His
people from their bondage in Egypt (Exod. 6:6), even as a
loyal kinsman cared for his own loved ones and rescued them
from danger. The psalmist sang the praises of the God "who
redeems your life from the pit" (Psalm 103:4*a*). So also
Hosea thought of salvation from death and Sheol as the re-
deeming work of God; he used this term in parallel with "ran-
som" in Hosea 13:14. A terrible captivity was foreseen by
the prophet Micah—the exile to Babylon—but the Lord
would rescue and "redeem [them] from the hand of [their]
enemies" (Mic. 4:10*b*). In the hearts of the New Testament disciples, the terms for redeem, redemption, and ran-
som express better than all others the atoning work of Christ.
Peter wrote: "You were not redeemed with perishable things
like silver or gold . . . but with precious blood, . . . the blood
of Christ" (1 Pet. 1:18-19).

We learn that not only the ten witnesses, called "the
elders" in 4:11, were watching the proceedings, but a crowd
of citizens of Bethlehem as well. All joined in with the cry
of approval, "We are witnesses" (4:11*a*). They then showed
their pleasure in the new development and pronounced their
blessing upon the marriage that was about to take place.
They must have admired Boaz for his integrity and kindness
to Ruth and Naomi, and they approved of Ruth for her faithfulness to her mother-in-law from the beginning. No higher
praise could be evoked than to compare Ruth to the "mothers

of Israel," Rachel and Leah. Little is known of Perez from the Bible record, except that he was the favored twin born to Judah and Tamar and the direct ancestor of Boaz (Gen. 38:29-30).

VI. The Marriage of Ruth and Boaz (4:13-17)

A great celebration must have taken place following the legal decision that gave Boaz the right of the "levirate" to marry Ruth. Such weddings in those days often lasted a week or longer, with feasting and joyful festivities for the entire community. Samson's wedding to the daughter of a Philistine at Timnah lasted seven days (Judg. 14:12), as we observed earlier. But the text moves on quickly to an event of even greater importance, the birth of a son to Ruth and Boaz.

Nothing could have confirmed and revealed the divine blessing on the union between Ruth and Boaz more fully than the birth of a male child. All children are a gift from the Lord of life and Creator of all that exists (see Gen. 4:1, 25; 1 Sam. 1:19-20), but a male child and heir was urgently needed to solve the problem faced by Naomi and Ruth. The son that was born, Obed, would become their "redeemer" (*goel*) in a different sense than that displayed by the actions of Boaz. The village women saw this fact and exclaimed, "Blessed is the Lord who has not left you without a redeemer [*goel*] today" (4:14b). By this grandson, Naomi would have provision for her old age, recompense for her losses, and the assurance that the good name of her deceased husband and sons would continue to be remembered. Obed was truly "a restorer of life," as 4:15a says. All who have experienced the redemption that is in Christ should echo Naomi's feelings of joy, for He is the Spring of all our joys and the Renewer of our hearts whenever we become despondent. With the psalmist, we lift our prayers to the Lord, because He is indeed our "Rock and [our] Redeemer" (Psalm 19: 14*b*).

As Naomi took over the care and nursing of her little grandson, Obed, whose name means "servant boy" in Hebrew, she once again assumed her own beautiful name of Naomi, "the pleasant one." A special prominence is given by the writer of Ruth to the women who surrounded Naomi in the narrative. Several times their voices and participation are recorded. In their minds, "A son has been born to Naomi," not to Ruth, since Naomi's need for the *goel* had been more urgent (4:17). Ruth, however, held their highest esteem. She "is better to you than seven sons," they exclaimed to Naomi (4:15*b*), recognizing also the love that so patently existed between the two women.

Mothers in Israel and in Jewish communities down through the centuries have always enjoyed a high place of praise and honor. Among them, none stand more beautifully for the ideals of fidelity and integrity than Naomi and Ruth.

VII. The Genealogy of David (4:18-22)

The language of these closing verses closely resembles that found in Genesis and Numbers, where genealogies are also cited. *Toledoth* (4:18) really represents a "history" or "account" rather than a list of names (cf. Gen. 2:4, first of ten instances in the book of Genesis).

Perez was a twin son born of Tamar to Judah, and he founded the main lineage of the tribe. His son *Hezron* was among the men of Judah who entered Egypt at the beginning of the sojourn (Gen. 46:12), although there is some indication that he may have actually been born in Egypt.

Ram is renamed *Aram* in the Septuagint and in Matthew 1:3, and his son *Amminadab* became the father-in-law of the high priest, Aaron (Exod. 6:23). According to this record of only four or five names, a number of generations are lacking to account for the total of 430 years in Egypt. It is obvious that lesser figures are not mentioned, and the list is cut to ten because of stylistic or practical considerations.

Nahshon was the head of the tribe of Judah during the first part of the wilderness wanderings (Num. 2:3). His son was *Salmon,* or *Salmah,* who became the husband of Rahab, the harlot of Jericho: "And to Salmon was born Boaz by Rahab; and to Boaz was born Obed" (Matt. 1:5*a*). Nothing explicitly indicates that gaps or missing names must be considered, yet the time from Salmon to Boaz requires that other forefathers be added to the genealogy to harmonize with the history of Judah as we know it.

Obed was David's grandfather, and *Jesse* stood between. All were men of honor, and most were citizens of the little village of Bethlehem. Matthew, whose genealogy agrees exactly with this one in Ruth, pointed to the Messiah's impeccable credentials: "Jesus Christ, the son of David, the son of Abraham" (1:1). One more time Bethlehem would produce a royal son: Jesus, born of the virgin Mary and heir to David's throne.

CONCLUSION

THE DAYS OF THE JUDGES ended with the great work and ministry of Samuel, whose life formed the final span in the bridge of mighty men between Moses and the monarchy. The narratives of those days of hardship have been told with candor and honesty; none of the ugly aspects have been hidden or altered to create an impression of well-being. The Lord's discipline and punishment of His people are as important to their history as His saving acts in answer to their prayers.

The Holy Spirit faithfully moved over the people of Israel and into the lives of her heroic leaders. By the Spirit of God, the judges performed miraculous deeds in the liberation and conservation of the tribes; certainly they did not triumph by their own ingenuity or strength. A lesson in the moral foundations of human history has been dramatized before us in these accounts from the perspective of the inspired prophet (whoever he was), who was used by the Spirit to record these books of Judges and Ruth.

The gracious act of Boaz to receive Ruth and provide for her family is the first and finest example of the Hebrew meaning of "redeemer" in all the Scriptures. From the beautiful union of Ruth and Boaz comes a deeper understanding of the relationship between Christ and the church. Finally, as the fruit of that union, we have the king "after God's own heart," the shepherd of Israel. To David God promised a royal lineage that would never end, and in David's son, the Messiah, our Lord, all the promises of the Bible come true.

SELECTED BIBLIOGRAPHY

Aharoni, Yohanon. *The Land of the Bible: A Historical Geography*. Philadelphia: Westminster, 1967.

Albright, William F. *Yahweh and the Gods of Canaan*. Garden City, N.Y.: Doubleday, 1969.

Baldwin, J. G. "Ruth." In *The New Bible Commentary: Revised*. Edited by Donald Guthrie and Alec Motyer. Grand Rapids: Eerdmans, 1970.

Boling, Robert G. *Judges*. The Anchor Bible. Garden City, N.Y.: Doubleday, 1969.

Bruce, F. F. "Judges." In *The New Bible Commentary: Revised*. Edited by Donald Guthrie and Alec Motyer. Grand Rapids: Eerdmans, 1970.

Burney, C. F. *The Book of Judges*. New York: Ktav, 1970.

Farrar, F. W. *The Book of Judges*. Layman's Handy Commentary Series. Grand Rapids: Zondervan, 1961.

Fausset, A. R. *A Critical and Expository Commentary on the Book of Judges*. 1885. Reprint. Minneapolis: James and Klock, 1977.

Geden, A. S. "Book of Judges." In *The International Standard Bible Encyclopaedia,* edited by James Orr. 5 vols. 1915. Reprint. Grand Rapids: Eerdmans, 1939. 3:1772-75.

Gray, John. *Joshua, Judges, and Ruth*. The Century Bible. Greenwood, S.C.: Attic, 1967.

Martin, J. D. *The Book of Judges*. Cambridge Bible Commentary Series. London: Cambridge U., 1962.

Payne, J. B. "Judges." In *New Bible Dictionary,* edited by J. D. Douglas. Grand Rapids: Eerdmans, 1962.

Pfeiffer, Charles. *Old Testament History*. Grand Rapids: Baker, 1973.

Thompson, J. A. *The Bible and Archaeology*. Devon, England: Paternoster, 1962.

Vaux, Roland de. *The Early History of Israel*. Philadelphia: Westminster, 1978.

Wiseman, D. J., ed. *Peoples of Old Testament Times*. Oxford: Oxford U., Clarendon, 1973.

Wright, G. E. *Biblical Archaeology*. Philadelphia: Westminster, 1957.

Moody Press, a ministry of the Moody Bible Institute, is designed for education, evangelization, and edification. If we may assist you in knowing more about Christ and the Christian life, please write us without obligation: Moody Press, c/o MLM, Chicago, Illinois 60610.